"In the desert prepare the way for the Lord; make straight in the wilderness a highway for our God."

"A virgin will be with child and will give birth to a son, and will call him Immanuel."

"His name shall be called wonderful. . . ."

"He was pierced for our transgressions, he was crushed for our iniquities. . . ."

"Though your sins are like scarlet, they shall be white as snow."

No wonder Isaiah's book has been called the "Old Testament Gospel." It comes to us from a man whose lips the Almighty God had touched with fire. "Tell them of my love for them," God said. "Tell them I will be their light in the darkness all around. You, Isaiah, must LIFT HIGH THE TORCH so that My people may see Me."

More than in any other Old Testament book, the prophecy of Isaiah brings us face to face with the Savior. He calls us, as He has called those in every century: "Come all you who are thirsty, come to the waters. . . ."

OTHER BIBLE ALIVE titles:

OLD TESTAMENT SURVEYS
Let Day Begin
Freedom Road
Years of Darkness, Days of Glory
Edge of Judgment
Springtime Coming

NEW TESTAMENT SURVEYS
The Servant King
The Great Adventure
Regions Beyond
Christ Preeminent
Pass It On
His Glory

LARRY RICHARDS
BIBLE ALIVE SERIES

Lift High the Torch

The Gospel in the Old Testament
Studies in Isaiah

David C. Cook Publishing Co.
ELGIN, ILLINOIS—WESTON, ONTARIO
FULLERTON, CALIFORNIA

Published by David C. Cook Publishing Co., 850 N. Grove Ave., Elgin, IL 60120
Edited by Sharrel Keyes
Cover photo by Ed Elsner
Printed in the United States of America
ISBN 0-89191-087-5

CONTENTS

Part One

VISIONS OF JUDGMENT
Isaiah 1—35

THE HOLY ONE

BOTH LOW AND HIGH will be humbled
   and the eyes of the arrogant will be brought low.
But the Lord Almighty will be exalted by his jus-
      tice,
   the holy God will show himself holy by his righ-
      teousness.

Isaiah 5:15-16

To the Jews, Isaiah was the greatest of the prophets. The commentator Delitzsch called Isaiah the "universal prophet."

Probably no Old Testament document has been more deeply studied than the Book of Isaiah. Certainly none has had more books and articles written about it. The New Testament alludes to it over two hundred fifty times and quotes it specifically at least fifty times.

There are several reasons for this fascination with

Isaiah. As literature, Isaiah has been called "the climax of Hebrew literary art." In content, it deals in a sweeping way with the great themes of the Old Testament. Judgment and hope, sin and redemption, find clear expression here. Christians have been fascinated by the picture of Jesus the Messiah drawn by this man who wrote so many centuries before Christ's birth. The picture of the suffering Messiah in Isaiah 53 has been critical in our understanding of Jesus' Calvary death.

Isaiah has also been a source of controversy. The book is divided into two distinct halves, set apart by a historical interlude. The first half of Isaiah announces judgment; the second half seems to assume the judgment has passed and that hope has come. Were these two sections of Isaiah written by the same person? Or was "Second Isaiah" added later on? In the main, conservatives have argued persuasively that the whole book was written by Isaiah the son of Amoz, whose ministry extended over some sixty years from 739 to about 681 B.C.

This was a critical period of Old Testament history. Israel, the Northern Kingdom, was overwhelmed by Assyria. Judah was threatened as well. What was God's message to a nation and people threatened by a great Gentile world power? How were His people (and how are we) to live in the face of the power of the world around them?

But the primary reason for reading Isaiah is to see the Lord. Certainly we've seen God in other Old Testament books. We've seen His power in the Exodus, His righteousness in the Law, His justice in the Book of Judges. But somehow it's as though we saw God *through* the events: He's there, but as a shadow; glimpsed, but not fully seen, in His actions in history. In Isaiah the veil of history is pulled aside and God is revealed in all His glory.

It's as if we set out at night to explore a new land, holding up our flickering candles to light the darkness. We see, but not clearly. And then torchlight more brilliant than the sun fills the sky, and what had been only outlines becomes solid and real. In the light of that torch, we see clearly for the first time. Isaiah's distinctive ministry is to lift high the torch, to show us, in brilliant clarity, the God men grope after.

For all of us who desire to know God in a deeper and fuller way, the Book of Isaiah holds great promise. As we study it together, we will be filled with wonder at the greatness and majesty of our God. We will be moved to praise and to hope, as God lifts high the torch of revelation to show us . . . Himself!

"I SAW THE LORD"
Isaiah 6

The year was 739 B.C. It was the twelfth year of Jotham's coregency, three years after the death of Israel's great king, Jeroboam II. According to tradition this may have been the actual year in which, on the banks of the Tiber River across the Mediterranean, Rome was founded.

In Judah it was the year that King Uzziah died.

For Isaiah it was the year he saw the Lord.

11

These events were turning points for both Judah and Isaiah. For Judah, Uzziah's death marked the beginning of the end of peace and prosperity. Assyria had begun to expand westward. Israel joined with Syria to stave off an attack and then tried to force Judah into a coalition with them against Assyria. Judah refused to go along, so Israel and Syria attempted to replace her king with a man of their own choosing. Finally, King Ahaz of Judah called on Assyria for support against his two local enemies, only to find himself threatened by this voracious helper. Ultimately, Israel became a puppet state and then suffered complete destruction (722 B.C.), and Judah was left exposed on her northern and western flanks.

Within the land there was a deepening spiritual decline. Uzziah had begun as a godly king, and "as long as he sought the Lord, God made him prosper" (2 Chron. 26: 5). Growing military success, however, made Uzziah proud. He turned away from God, was struck with leprosy, and retired to a separate house for his final years. Jotham, his son, ruled for him. He "did what was right in the eyes of the Lord" (2 Chron. 27: 2) and during his sixteen-year reign enjoyed continued political and military success. But he had little influence on the practices of Judah's people. The Bible tells us that they "still followed corrupt practices" (2 Chron. 27: 2). The sins against which Isaiah cried out were deeply entrenched in the life-style of Judah as well as Israel.

Uzziah's death was symbolic. He who had begun so well and had found prosperity in obedience had been struck by the dread disease of leprosy. An appearance of health and strength would remain for a time, but the disease was at work within the body of the king; its marks would become more and more visible as the ravages of that dread sickness took their toll. Finally, destroyed within and without, Uzziah would die; his pride and disobedience brought judgment on him.

Isaiah pointed out that Judah was also diseased because she had left the Lord:

Ah, sinful nation,
   a people loaded with guilt,
a brood of evildoers,
   children given to corruption.
They have forsaken the Lord;
   they have spurned the Holy One of Israel
   and turned their backs on him.

Isaiah 1:4

He graphically describes the advanced stages of leprosy,

Your whole head is injured,
   your whole heart afflicted.
From the sole of your foot to the top of your head
   there is no soundness—
only wounds and welts
   and open sores,
not cleansed or bandaged
   or soothed with oil.

Isaiah 1:5-6

13

Judah's sickness, like that of Uzziah's, must end in death. The year Uzziah died was a pivotal time for Judah. She had a last opportunity to choose between life and death. And Judah's choice, like his, had been made.

Yet this was the year Isaiah saw the Lord!

We read about his vision in chapter 6 and recognize that the prophet has been called to a lifelong work. From this time on, Isaiah would lift high the torch to reveal God to his people. He would proclaim the God who stands behind all history, the God who wants us to know and love Him. In the year Uzziah died, Isaiah saw the Lord, and his whole life and perspective were transformed ... as ours can be.

The description (6:1-4). Perhaps Isaiah had come to the Temple to pray or offer sacrifices. We're not told. All we know is that suddenly the veils were stripped away and Isaiah "saw the Lord seated on a throne, high and exalted" (v. 1). He was surrounded by angelic beings. The foundation shook, smoke filled the Temple, and God's brilliance blazed as the beings cried out:

> Holy, holy, holy is the Lord Almighty;
> the whole earth is full of his glory.
>
> *Isaiah 6:3*

Isaiah was filled with dread. He was confronted with the fact about God that his people had forgotten: the God of Israel is holy.

Isaiah's response (6:5-9). When Isaiah saw God's holiness, he also saw his own condition. With all his

14

pride and self-righteousness stripped away, Isaiah cried, "Woe is me! . . . I am ruined! For I am a man of unclean lips, and I live among a people of unclean lips" (v. 5). Against the stark holiness of God, Isaiah suddenly saw his whole life-style as a perhaps unwitting but nevertheless real expression of an inner wickedness.

But then God acted. One of the angelic beings touched Isaiah's lips with a live coal from the altar, announcing, "Your guilt is taken away and your sin atoned for" (v. 7). The altar fires, which would one day flare up with Jesus' blood, now brought Isaiah's covering from sin and release from guilt. Pronounced holy by the Holy One, Isaiah could now stand before the Lord.

Then God's voice was heard where before only the voice of the angel had echoed. "Whom shall I send? And who will go for us?"

Isaiah immediately responds: "Here I am. Send me!" (v. 8).

Isaiah's commission. Isaiah is now charged with a staggering task. He is to speak God's Word to a people who have made an irrevocable choice and warn them of the certainty of judgment. He is to point out their blindness and their unwillingness to listen. Isaiah has to face the fact that God's people will remain deaf and blind to the Lord's message for another hundred years

until the cities lie ruined
and without inhabitant,
until the houses are left deserted

15

and the fields ruined and ravaged;
until the Lord has sent everyone far away,
and the land is utterly forsaken.

Isaiah 6:11-12

Only then will God's people finally hear. Only then will they read the words of Isaiah the prophet and see the Holy One who reveals sin and brings forgiveness.

What a burden for Isaiah to bear. He knows the men and women he walks beside are doomed; he realizes the supernatural power with which his words are endowed and all his prayer concern will never break through the hardened hearts of his generation. But what a blessing to know that another day will come! Someday, when Isaiah himself has been laid to rest and all the people who spurn God have returned to dust, other generations will pore over Isaiah's words and find God's Spirit quickening them to life with the Holy One of Israel.

And so it happened. Isaiah prophesied judgment, and it came. But generations of believers before Christ pored over Isaiah's words and found a vital hope. And generations after Christ have returned to this book to renew their vision of the Lord.

One exciting archaeological find, the Dead Sea Scrolls, gives us insight into how accurately the prophet's words have been preserved. The Qumran community hid their sacred library some 180 years before Christ. These were discovered in 1947. Apparently Isaiah, along with Deuteronomy and Psalms, were especially loved by these Old Testa-

16

ment believers. Among the finds was a copy of Isaiah, the first copy of any Old Testament book from a pre-Christian time. Before this time our earliest text of the Hebrew Bible dated from around A.D. 1100. The striking fact is that the text of the scroll authenticates the Hebrew text of our Bible; except for minor differences in vocalization, spelling, and the presence or absence of an article ("the," "that"), this ancient text is the same as the text of some thirteen thousand years later! God has preserved across the centuries an accurate text of His Word so you and I could read our Old Testament with the confidence that what we see on the pages is a translation of the very words the authors penned.

THREE SERMONS
Isaiah 1–5

These first chapters of Isaiah are three sermons that together give us a picture of Isaiah's early ministry. They also underline the holiness theme that culminates in Isaiah 6. Each sermon gives us insight into the spiritual condition of God's people, a condition of great concern to the Holy God.

An indictment (Isa. 1). This first sermon is both an indictment and an appeal in which God describes the sins that characterize the life-style of His people. In choosing the way of sin, Judah has "spurned the Holy One of Israel" (v. 4). Living in sin is an act of rebellion, a deliberate choice to turn against God.

God's complaint against Israel focuses on her lack of concern with justice. Isaiah cries out to them,

17

Your hands are full of blood;
    wash and make yourselves clean.
Take your evil deeds
    out of my sight!
Stop doing wrong,
    learn to do right!
Pursue justice,
    encourage the oppressed.
Defend the cause of the fatherless,
    plead the case of the widow.

Isaiah 1:16-17

Judah still maintained the appearance of religion. She continued to worship; offered sacrifices; held sabbaths, solemn convocations, required festivals, and appointed feasts. But her heart was far from God; her life was, in fact, dedicated to ungodliness. God says Judah must be purged so that once again Jerusalem may be known as the City of Righteousness.

Zion will be redeemed with justice,
    her penitent ones with righteousness.
But rebels and sinners will both be broken to-
        gether,
    and those who forsake the Lord will perish.

Isaiah 1:27-28

A description of judgment (Isa. 2–4). Isaiah sees beyond time to the end of history when the glory God intends for His purified and holy people (2:2-5; 4:2-6) will be theirs. The promise is full of beauty.

18

God will judge between the nations; swords will be beaten into plowshares and spears into pruning hooks. No more will men train for war. The Lord will wash, cleanse, and shelter. Jerusalem will become "a refuge and hiding place from the storm and rain" (4: 6).

But before that time will be judgment!

> The Lord Almighty has a day in store
> for all the proud and lofty . . . .
> The arrogance of man will be brought low
> and the pride of men humbled. . . .
> Men will flee to caves in the rocks
> and to holes in the ground
> from the dread of the Lord
> and the splendor of his majesty,
> when he rises to shake the earth.
>
> *Isaiah 2:12, 17, 19*

The prosperity Judah has come to trust will be stripped away. Those who have crushed their brothers and ground down the faces of the poor will experience the full meaning of being crushed and ground down.

Judgment vindicated (Isa. 5). A farmer planted grapes, intending to receive a crop of choice fruit. But in spite of all the farmer's care, the yield was only sour and bitter grapes.

Applying the figure, Isaiah confronts the people of Judah. They are God's tender plantings, but the fruit they have brought forth is bitter. That was not the harvest God desired:

19

"He looked for justice, but saw bloodshed;
for righteousness, but heard cries of distress!"
Isaiah 5:7

So God will act to vindicate his holiness. He will not permit the people called by His name to tarnish His glory or spatter His character with their filth.

The Lord Almighty will be exalted by his justice, the Holy God will show himself holy by his righteousness.
Isaiah 5:16

Those who have rejected the word of the Lord will feel his anger burn and see His hand raised to strike.

Then comes the report of Isaiah's personal experience with God in chapter 6. Isaiah too saw the Holy One of Israel. But, unlike Judah, Isaiah dropped to his knees and confessed his sinfulness. Unlike Judah, Isaiah felt the burning touch of forgiveness, which did not bring pain but healing and a renewed relationship with God.

What a portrait for us. God comes to us as the Holy One. We can fall to our knees before God, acknowledging our sin, and discover that holiness heals. Or we can turn our backs on the vision as Judah did, and know that in spurning the Holy God we invite a dreadful, certain fate. For God *will* be exalted. The Holy God *will* show Himself holy. In forgiveness or in judgment, God's holiness is revealed.

How then will His holiness be revealed in me?

GOING DEEPER

Each chapter of this book is designed to orient you to a section of God's Word. You'll benefit most from these studies if you move from reading the chapter into a direct Bible study experience. The *Going Deeper* questions at the end of each chapter will guide you in that personal Bible study.

to personalize
1. Select one of the three sermons to read and study as follows:
- Isaiah 1: What specifically does this chapter identify as unholiness? How do you think God would describe a holy life-style?
- Isaiah 2—4. Describe what God is straining to accomplish among us (Isa. 2: 1-5 and 4: 2-6). Look at the rest of the sermon. What in man's life-style blocks that goal of cleansing and peace? What actions will God take against such behavior?
- Isaiah 5: Imagine yourself to be a contemporary of Isaiah. How many excuses could you find for your behavior? What objections would you raise to Isaiah's portrait of coming judgment? How does Isaiah 5 answer these objections and vindicate God's judgment?

2. Isaiah's writings are full of timeless expressions of great comfort and value to believers. For instance, this word in the middle of judgment is encouraging for all individuals who live in a sin-marred society: "Tell the righteous that it shall be well with them, for

they will enjoy the fruit of their deeds" (Isa. 3:10).
Select one short passage to memorize this week and
continue to memorize a section from each of your
coming studies:

● Isa. 1:18-19　　　● Isa. 2:5　　　● Isa. 5:16

3. Read Isaiah 6:1-9. What is God saying *to you* in
this passage?

to probe

1. This chapter discussed the long-standing controversy over the unity of the Book of Isaiah. Research several books (from both conservative and
"critical" perspectives) and write a three- to five-
page paper on "The Two Isaiahs."

2. The Dead Sea Scrolls were a significant archaeological find. Read at least one book on these
scrolls, and write a brief report.

THE SOVEREIGN LORD

THE LORD ALMIGHTY is the one you are to regard as
    holy,
  he is the one you are to fear,
  he is the one you are to dread.
And he will be a sanctuary,
  but for both houses of Israel he will be
a stone that causes men to stumble
  and a rock that makes them fall,
and for the people of Jerusalem he will be
  a trap and a snare.
Many of them will stumble;
  they will fall and be broken,
  and be snared and be captured.
Isaiah 8:13-15

Isaiah tells us very little of himself. He will only say
that he and his children are signs to Israel from the
Lord (8:18). The prophet, after the brief but reveal-
ing picture of his call, submerges himself in his message and tells us nothing about his own feelings.
When we meet him next, holding his infant son

Shear-Jashub in his arms, he is confronting King Ahaz outside Jerusalem. Even the name of his son is a message: it means "a remnant will return" (7: 3).

AHAZ

Jotham, son of Uzziah, ruled for some sixteen years and then was succeeded by his son, Ahaz. While Jotham had followed the Lord's ways, Ahaz "did not do what was right in the eyes of the Lord" (2 Chron. 28: 1). He adopted the apostate ways and faith of the Northern Kingdom, Israel, even erecting images of Baal and sacrificing his own sons in the fire.

Politically, the times of Ahaz were marked by constant crisis. Tiglath-pileser, ruler of Assyria, was expanding his power westward. Egypt, which had counterbalanced the power of northern empires for centuries, was now weak. Syria and the Northern Kingdom, Israel, were struggling to form a defensive alliance against the Assyrian encroachment. Ahaz was pressured to join the coalition. He refused.

Determined to replace Ahaz with a puppet king who would cooperate with them, Rezin of Syria (whose capital was Damascus) and Pekah of Israel (whose capital was Samaria) (7: 8-9) decided to attack Judah. They forced Ahaz's hand, and he sent envoys to Assyria begging for help against his nearby enemies. This was all the excuse Assyria needed. Soon the Middle East was plunged into a complex and fratricidal war.

The first action was a battle between Judah and

the combined powers of Israel and Syria. In a crushing defeat some one hundred twenty thousand of Judah's soldiers were killed. Another two hundred thousand women and children were taken captive but, through the intervention of a prophet sent by God (see 2 Chron. 28: 8-15), they were released and returned to Judah.

When Assyria responded to Ahaz's plea for help, she swept down to crush both Damascus and Samaria, and then turned on Judah, her ally! Tiglath-pileser came against Ahaz and "afflicted him instead of strengthening him" (2 Chron. 28:20). Ahaz was forced to strip the land of its wealth to buy off Assyria (2 Chron. 28:21), and Judah became in effect a satellite nation that reflected the policy of its powerful neighbor.

Bitterly angry at God, Ahaz closed the Jerusalem Temple, stripped it of its remaining treasures, and cut up even the golden vessels dedicated to God's worship. He "sacrificed to the gods of Damascus which had defeated him and said, 'Because the gods of the kings of Syria helped them, I will sacrifice to them that they may help me' " (2 Chron. 28:23).

THE PROMISE
Isaiah 7

Before the days of battle came, God sent Isaiah with his infant son Shear-Jashub to meet Ahaz "at the end of the aqueduct of the Upper Pool, on the road to the Washerman's Field." He was to review the political situation and warn Ahaz of the danger from Judah's neighbors. God was still the Sovereign Lord, while Judah's enemies were mere men. God promises, "It will not take place, it will not happen," but goes on to warn, "If you do not stand firm in your faith, you will not stand at all" (7: 7, 9). The plot to replace Ahaz came to nothing. Judah was defeated, but Ahaz remained king.

The sign (Isa. 7:10-14). God then instructed Ahaz to ask for a sign.

God had indicated ways that a prophet's message could be tested. The Hebrew prophet was to speak in the name of the Lord (not in the name of a false god), and his word was to *invariably come true.* If the word did not come true, or the foretold event did not happen, that person was not a true prophet (see Deut. 18: 17-22).

But what of a prophet who foretells a distant event that may take place long after he and his listeners have died? It was common in such a case for the prophet also to speak of contemporary things, so that the message could be authenticated as from God. Elijah's warning to King Ahab of a coming drought was confirmed by the Lord in just such a manner (see 1 Kings 17—18).

Isaiah's demand that Ahaz ask for a sign, then, was not unusual. But Ahaz replied, "I will not ask; I will not put the Lord to the test" (v. 12). At first this reply seems almost pious; but it is hardly that. Not only was Ahaz insincere in his mocking quotation of Deuteronomy 6: 16, he was also disobeying a direct command of God through His prophet. We can't hear the sneer that undoubtedly filled this apostate

26

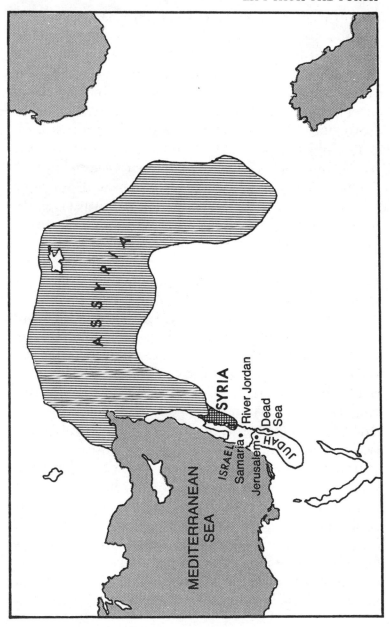

king's voice with mockery, but we can recognize Isaiah's sharp rebuke: "Is it not enough to try the patience of men? Will you try the patience of my God also?" (7:13). In anger Isaiah goes on to announce a sign, but a sign that will only come long after Judah lies broken under the enemy: "The Lord himself will give you a sign: A virgin will be with child and will give birth to a son, and will call him Immanuel" (7:14). The name *Immanuel* means "God with us!"

God is determined to act in human history. Petty kings' dreams of conquest, or their fears for preservation are meaningless. One day the true King, God Himself, will take on human form. When God becomes man *with us,* then the fears of Ahaz and all the glory of the kingdoms of this world will dissolve in the revelation of true glory. The King will enter history as a man, born of a virgin. When He, the ultimate sign, appears, all nations will recognize the majesty and wisdom of the Sovereign God.

The judgment (Isaiah 7:15-25). When will the Immanuel come? Isaiah sets no date, but he does know that before the promised child is weaned (7:15), the two nations Ahaz fears most will be laid waste and Judah herself will undergo a time of destruction from Assyria, the one on whom Ahaz had pinned his hopes! (7:17). By refusing to remain still and trust in God, Ahaz will initiate a chain of events that will bring Assyria and devastating judgment upon Palestine. Poverty will replace plenty. Briars and thorns will grow in the once-cultivated fields. Assyria will carry off Israel into captivity while Judah is beaten down. But even this terror will not cure Judah or bring her back to God. Finally, when Babylon has conquered Assyria, Judah will face captivity.

THE TWO KINGDOMS

In reading Isaiah it's important to remember that the Hebrew people were divided into two nations, a northern kingdom (Israel) and a southern (Judah), which was Isaiah's home. Although God spoke through Isaiah *about* the Northern Kingdom and, indeed, all the surrounding powers, Isaiah's ministry remained directed to Judah. Israel had had a succession of evil kings; not one godly man broke the pattern. Judah had seen revival under kings such as Asa and Jehoshaphat.

The fate of Israel stood as a vivid object lesson to Judah. If Judah were to choose the evil ways of her sister Israel, her fate must surely be the same. Judah was warned when Sargon tore the Israelites from the Promised Land in 722 B.C. God had demonstrated His principles of judgment in an unmistakable way. Now God's warnings to Judah would come to pass just as his pronouncements against the Northern Kingdom did. History would bear terrible testimony to the trustworthiness of God's Word.

How carefully then Judah should heed every message. How quickly Judah should repent, but, in spite of all the evidence, Judah *would not*. She saw, but she did not perceive. She heard, but she would not listen. Like her king, Judah would choose to spurn God's offer of a sign.

THE IMMEDIATE FUTURE
Isaiah 8

Now Isaiah and his wife have another son, named Maher-Shalal-Hash-Baz. The name means "Quick to the plunder, swift to the spoil," and points to the impending judgment on Israel. Before this boy could talk, Syria and Israel were crushed, their capitals plundered, their people deported. The armies of Assyria flowed over the borders of Judah to flood the nation, rising swiftly from feet to knees to waist and shoulders, right up to the very head itself, Jerusalem. The waters would recede, but Judah was left a disaster (8: 6-10).

The people of God needed to forget their fear of men, of Rezin and Pekah who terrorized Ahaz but who soon were to die, and to fear instead the God who judges iniquity. Isaiah cries out,

> The Lord Almighty is the one you are to regard as
>   holy,
>   he is the one you are to fear,
>   he is the one you are to dread.
> *Isaiah 8:13*

He would be a sanctuary to any who would return to Him, but if they refuse to return, the God they spurn will bring about their brokenness. Yet instead of turning to God, the people turn to mediums and spiritists, to consult the dead on behalf of the living (8: 11-22).

THE FIXED PURPOSE
Isaiah 9:1-7

In spite of the coming disaster, God's intention to bless His people and bring them holiness has not changed. One day the promised child will be born. One day the promised Son will be given. He, whose names are Wonderful Counselor, Mighty God, Everlasting Father, and Prince of Peace, will reign on the Davidic throne over a cleansed world.

> Of the extension of his government and peace
>   there will be no end.
> He will reign on David's throne,
>   and over his kingdom,
> establishing and upholding it
>   with justice and righteousness
>   from that time on and forever.
> The zeal of the Lord Almighty
>   will accomplish this.

Isaiah 9:7

On the throne where Ahaz, that unworthy descendant of David now sits, another King will reign. He will establish the righteousness and justice that Ahaz's every act denies. And of that kingdom there will be no end.

HISTORY INTERVENES
Isaiah 9:8–10:34

Before the final kingdom comes, much history

31

will intervene. And the course of history, as well as its appointed end, is fixed by the Sovereign Lord. Israel and its capital Samaria will be destroyed by its enemies.

> Yet for all this, his anger is not turned away,
> his hand is still upraised.
>
> *Isaiah 9:12*

The elders and the prominent men who led Israel into sin, and the prophets who lied for them, will be killed.

> Yet for all this, his anger is not turned away,
> his hand is still upraised.
>
> *Isaiah 9:17*

Those who have defrauded the poor and made unjust laws for their own profit will lose all their wealth and cringe among the captives, or fall among the slain.

> Yet for all this, his anger is not turned away,
> his hand is still upraised.
>
> *Isaiah 10:4*

Then, when judgment has been executed to the full, God will judge the persecutors! God has given Assyria power to be the disciplining rod against the Lord's willful people. But Assyria will fail to recognize God, so she must suffer punishment "for the willful pride of [her] heart and the haughty look in

[her] eyes" (10:12). God will be recognized, finally, as the Holy One of Israel.

And now, in the quietness following judgment's raging storm, the remnant looks up and at last sees God. How great a day when they "will truly rely on the Lord, the Holy One of Israel" (10:20).

In the end, the powers of this world will be lopped off like branches, and the burden will be lifted from the shoulders of God's people. In the end, history will turn to destiny, and the plans and promises of our Sovereign Lord will be perfectly fulfilled.

GOING DEEPER

to personalize

1. What do you think Isaiah intended us to gain from his portrait of God as Sovereign Lord? What does this portrait of God say to *you?*

2. Choose one of the following to study in-depth:

● Isaiah 8. We've seen in Isaiah 1 and 5 the response God calls us to make to each other. What response are we to make to *Him?*

● Isaiah 9:8—10:19. Have you ever thought of the meaning of God's anger? What does this passage tell you about it?

● Isaiah 9:1-7; 10:20-34. God's promise of destiny has great meaning for all mankind. How are we to live while awaiting it?

3. To memorize for personal enrichment:

● Isa. 8:12-13
● Isa. 9:6-7
● Isa. 10:20

to probe

1. Research in a concordance the name Almighty God. With what acts of God is this name associated?

2. There has been much controversy over the meaning of the word in 7:14 translated "virgin" in the NIV and "young woman" in the RSV. The word, *alma,* is used six times in the Old Testament and never of a married woman. It is translated in the Septuagint (the pre-Christian Greek translation of the Old Testament) by the word *parthenos* (meaning "virgin") and is so quoted in the New Testament as well.

Research this question yourself and write briefly on the implications of the word chosen to translate *alma.*

3

Isaiah 11–24

GOD, THE JUDGE

HE WILL NOT JUDGE by what he sees with his eyes
    or decide by what he hears with his ears;
but with righteousness he will judge the needy,
    with justice he will give decisions for the poor of
    the earth.
He will strike the earth with the rod of his mouth;
    with the breath of his lips he will slay the wicked.
Righteousness will be his belt
    and faithfulness the sash around his waist.
Isaiah 11:3-5

We may find it hard to be comfortable with God when He reveals Himself as Judge. We have experienced inequities in our judicial system, and we've been bombarded with rationalizations that seek to establish one set of laws for the influential and another for the have-nots. Our sense of justice has become warped.

A recent article on white-collar crime quoted several businessmen and lawyers who had been sentenced to prison for frauds involving hundreds of thousands of dollars. These men argued bitterly that, for them, the shame of exposure was enough; certainly they did not deserve imprisonment like common criminals!

Too often the newspapers report a rape case brought to trial in which the victim becomes the defendant on the witness stand, subject to insinuations that she invited the crime against her.

Of course, we must have due process of law, and sometimes even the guilty will be set free on a technicality. After all, in an imperfect society, we cannot always be certain about guilt. Human eyes and ears are not always reliable witnesses. Perhaps more importantly, human emotions make us anything but impartial. Because it is so hard to be objective and never to waver from an absolute standard of righteousness, we find it difficult to accept the judicial system of the Sovereign Lord, who is *absolutely* just.

JUSTICE

We can't read the Old Testament without becoming convinced that God cares about all people and that He expresses His concern by a deep commitment to justice. Justice is hardly an abstract code. The Law of God has always been associated not with arbitrary rules but with life and with how people can best express love for each other.

God's concern for all people is clear in this sampling of Levitical law:

When you reap the harvest of your land, you shall not reap your field to its very border, neither shall you gather the gleanings after you harvest. And you shall not strip your vineyard bare, neither shall you gather the fallen grapes of your vineyard; you shall leave them for the poor and for the sojourner: I am the Lord your God.

You shall not steal, nor deal falsely, nor lie to one another. . . .

You shall not oppress your neighbor or rob him. The wages of a hired servant shall not remain with you all night until the morning. You shall not curse the deaf or put a stumbling block before the blind, but you shall fear your God: I am the Lord.

You shall do no injustice in judgment; you shall not be partial to the poor or defer to the great, but in righteousness shall you judge your neighbor . . . .

. . . You shall not take vengeance or bear any grudge against the sons of your own people, but you shall love your neighbor as yourself: I am the Lord.

Leviticus 19:9-18

Against the backdrop of the good and just life God planned for His people, Isaiah exposes the corrupt life-style of Israel and Judah.

The vineyard of the Lord Almighty
   is the house of Israel,
and the men of Judah

are the garden of his delight.
And he looked for justice, but saw bloodshed;
for righteousness, but heard cries of distress!

Isaiah 5:7

God has determined to bring terrible judgments on His people. But His actions throughout history have never been vindictive, nor have they been primarily deterrent; rather, they have been acts of *judgment.* God's goal is that justice may be established.

MESSIAH
Isaiah 11–12

Violence had become the life-style of Israel and Judah as well as the surrounding nations. As we remember Ahaz sacrificing his own sons to pagan gods, we can more easily accept the picture of God trampling out the grapes of wrath in His holy anger against such bestial sins. So, lest we forget what is really involved in the events Isaiah portrays, we are shown *Messiah.*

Messiah's person (Isa. 11:1-3). The house of David was a "lofty tree" felled by judgments of the Lord. From the stump (note: Jesse was David's father) springs a branch (an Old Testament symbol of the promised Messiah). God's own Spirit will fill Him with wisdom, understanding counsel, power, and knowledge. He will be in complete harmony with the holy character of God.

Messiah's task (Isa. 11:3-5). The task of this one

38

sent from God is to judge. Edward Young comments,

> The principle function of a ruler is to judge, and to reign with authority. How will this King, one who so delights in the fear of Yahweh, carry out His function of judging? To ask that question is to answer it, for His judging will be completely unlike that of previous rulers on David's throne. His judgment will not be based upon the ordinary sources of information open to men, namely, what men see and what they hear. Such means, the eyes and the ears, can bring at best an outward impression. For absolute justice, there must be absolute knowledge.[1]

When God acts in judgment He sees perfectly into the heart of every man and into the heart of every issue. Remembering it is God who is the Judge, we must forever turn our thoughts away from the temptation to judge Him!

Isaiah reassures us concerning the Messiah-Judge: "Righteousness will be his belt and faithfulness the sash around his waist" (11: 5). Archaeology tells us what this description means. In biblical times wrestlers wore belts. The object of a match was for each opponent to seek to wrest the other's belt away. Later, the figure of the belted man came to indicate any person ready to face a contest or engage in a struggle.

Isaiah pictures the poor and needy of the land moaning on the mat, as human arrogance and pride bruise the neck with a cruel boot. Man is no match for sin and injustice. But wait! Stepping into the arena comes a man belted for battle. His belt is woven of the duel strands of righteousness and faithfulness. No man or demon will ever snatch that belt from Him.

Restoration (Isa. 11:6-9). Now follows one of the most famous and moving of all passages of Scripture. After the judgment battle, when the Messiah has won His victory, righteousness and peace will be restored.

> The wolf will live with the lamb,
>   the leopard will lie down with the goat,
> the calf and the lion and the yearling together;
>   and a little child will lead them. . . .
> the lion will eat straw like the ox.
>   The infant will play near the hole of the
>   cobra. . . .
> They will neither harm nor destroy
>   in all my holy mountain,
> for the earth will be full of the knowledge of the
>   Lord
> as the waters cover the sea.
>
> *Isaiah 11:6-9*

The Gentiles (Isa. 11:10-16). In the days following Messiah's judgment victories, the hostility between Judah and Israel will be healed and all God's people will rally to Him. From every nation to which judgment has scattered them, the chosen of God will return to experience the blessings of Messianic rule.

Songs of praise (Isa. 12:1-6). This chapter contains two brief psalms. When God's judgment work is done and sin has tasted final defeat, how God's people will rejoice and sing His praise!

ORACLES OF DARKNESS
Isaiah 14–24

I'm writing this in a hotel in the city of Hilo, Hawaii. It's eight in the morning. Outside my window the heavy overcast has parted briefly, and the brilliant sunlight of Polynesia splashes through.

And now, just as quickly, the clouds close in again. The sunlight is gone; all seems dull and gray. And yet I know that above the clouds blocking my view is a radiance that warms and glows.

Isaiah 11 and 12 are like that flash of sunlight breaking through surrounding clouds. Seen from the perspective of the earthbound, Isaiah's portrait of judgment is dark indeed. But we have seen the purpose of God in the judgments He ordains. We have seen His battle belt of faithfulness and righteousness; we have caught a glimpse of the endless peace His final victory will win. We must remember the sunlight of that vision as we walk now under the lowering clouds, hearing words such as these:

The rising sun will be darkened,
   and the moon will not give its light.
I will punish the world for its evil,
   the wicked for their sins.
I will put an end to the arrogance of the haughty
   and will humble the pride of the ruthless.
Isaiah 13:10-11

41

The shouts of joy over your ripened fruit
  and over your harvests have been stilled.
Joy and gladness are gone from the orchards;
  no one sings or shouts in the vineyards;
no one treads out wine at the presses,
  for I have put an end to the shouting.
                                    Isaiah 16:9-10

See, the Lord is going to lay waste the earth
  and devastate it;
he will ruin its face
  and scatter its inhabitants—
it will be the same
  for priest as for people. . . .
The earth will be completely laid waste
  and totally plundered.
    The Lord has spoken this word.
                                    Isaiah 24:1-3

The oracles. We have now come to a series of divine declarations, or oracles, concerning surrounding nations. The great world powers of Isaiah's day (and coming powers like that of Babylon) who have set themselves against God will be themselves set aside as God's judgment brings them low. Only the righteous Kingdom of the Messiah will remain.

God raised these nations up to be instruments of judgment against His people (5:26-30; 7:18-20). Now Isaiah identifies these powers and exposes their sin. They have arrogantly gone beyond God's boundaries in punishing Israel. Even Babylon, which will fulfill the course begun by Assyria, will be

THE ORACLES

Isa. 13:1—14:23	Against Babylon
Isa. 14:24-27	Against Assyria
Isa. 14:28-32	Against Philistia
Isa. 15—16	Against Moab
Isa. 17	Against Damascus
Isa. 18	Against Cush
Isa. 19	Against Egypt
Isa. 20	Against Egypt and Cush
Isa. 21:1-10	Against Babylon
Isa. 21:11-12	Against Edom
Isa. 21:13-17	Against Arabia
Isa. 22	About Jerusalem
Isa. 23	About Tyre
Isa. 24	Portrait of judgments

unable to stand. All worldly powers directed against God and His purposes will be cut off.

Those who deny the possibility of prophetic foreknowledge argue that the name *Babylon* was substituted for *Assyria* by some later scribe. Those who believe the prophet was inspired by God understand that Babylon would consummate the scattering of God's people begun by Assyria.

Two elements of this prophecy have drawn much attention. Many have seen in the destruction of the boastful king (14:12-21) a portrait of Satan's fall from heaven (Luke 10:18). Of one thing we can be sure. *Every* arrogant power, whether in Satan, in kings, in you or me, that exalts itself against God . . . falls under sure judgment.

43

Another element deserving comment is the picture of a deserted Babylon. "She will never be inhabited," declares Isaiah,

> or lived in through all generations;
> no Arab will pitch his tent there,
>   no shepherd will rest his flocks there.
> But desert creatures will lie there,
>   owls will fill her houses . . . .
> Hyenas will howl in her strongholds,
>   jackals in her luxurious palaces.
>
> *Isaiah 13:20-22*

Today there is only an empty wilderness where Babylon once stood. The Lord is a great judge, and His judgment is sure.

About Egypt (Isa. 19). God's judgment is not only sure, it is purposive. After judgment, God brings restoration and healing.

> In that day there will be an altar to the Lord in the heart of Egypt . . . . The Lord will make himself known to the Egyptians, and in that day they will acknowledge the Lord . . . . They will turn to the Lord, and he will respond to their pleas and heal them.
>
> *Isaiah 19:19-22*

However stern the judgment of God seems, however terrible the vision of God as Judge may be, behind the darkened clouds the sun of blessing shines.

GOING DEEPER

to personalize

1. Study carefully Isaiah 11—12. What is the purpose for a criminal-justice system in society? Is it prevention? Retribution? Punishment? Rehabilitation? Or something else? Can you see any guidelines in the Bible's portrait of God as Judge?

2. Select any two of the oracles (see list on page 43) to study carefully.

3. Isaiah 24 summarizes God's judgment. Read this chapter. How does the writer feel, knowing that judgment draws close to him and his people?

4. Here are several passages you may wish to commit to memory.

- Isa. 11:1-3
- Isa. 12:1-3
- Isa. 13:9-11

- Isa. 14:26-27
- Isa. 16:4-5
- Isa. 24:21-23

to probe

1. Specific prophecies are made in this passage about both Babylon and Tyre. See if you can trace in commentaries how (or if) these have been fulfilled.

2. Does the famous Isaiah 14:11-15 passage describe the sin of Satan that led to his fall? What commentators (from Tertullian on) have thought so? What are their reasons? What do you think after your research?

3. Trace through Scripture the judgment acts of God. Then write a careful description of God as Judge. What principles does He operate by? What are His motives and goals? How does judgment ex-

press His essential character? How are His people called to exercise similar judgment? This can be a major project, and a very helpful one for you.

1. Edward Young, *The Book of Isaiah*, 3 vols. (Grand Rapids: Eerdmans, 1965), 1:383-84.

GOD, OUR SALVATION

WE HAVE A STRONG CITY;
  God makes salvation
  its walls and ramparts.
Open the gates
  that the righteous nation may enter,
  the nation that keeps faith.
You will keep in perfect peace
  him whose mind is steadfast,
  because he trust in you.
Trust in the Lord forever,
  for the Lord, the Lord, is the Rock eternal.
Isaiah 26:1-4

I was a young teenager walking home after a high-school game. Clouds hid the moon, and a damp breeze cut through my thin jacket. Just as I reached the flowerbed bordering our yard, I felt a jolt of terror.

Out of the total black of the peony bushes a mysterious shape rose with a deep, threatening rumble. I jerked back, poised to run, and then I recognized him! It was my own dog, Ezra! Half asleep, he'd failed to recognize me and had risen stiff-legged and growling. In the dark I'd failed to recognize him as well. What a relief for each of us to recognize the other as his own!

In a way, that incident gives us a clue to understanding this section of Isaiah's book. God has risen as a dark specter, a strange and terrifying shadow. Every way Isaiah has described God—the Holy One, the Sovereign Lord, the great Judge—has promised sure judgment. But Israel has not recognized nor claimed relationship with the God Isaiah knows.

God will not always remain a stranger. The judgment about to come upon His people will work a fundamental change in them.

A GOD TO BE TRUSTED
Isaiah 25–27

The first words of Isaiah 25 introduce, for the first time, a tone of *personal relationship*. God's people respond to Him, saying,

> Surely this is our God;
>   we trusted in him, and he saved us.
> This is the Lord, we trusted in him;
>   let us rejoice and be glad in his salvation.
> > *Isaiah 25:9*

The people delight in their new relationship:

48

Yes, Lord, walking in the way of your laws,
  we wait for you;
your name and renown
  are the desires of our hearts. . . .
Lord, you establish peace for us;
  all that we have accomplished you have done
    for us.
O Lord, our God, other lords besides you have
    ruled over us,
  but your name alone do we honor.

Isaiah 26:8, 12-13

In these chapters we see Judah recognizing God for the first time as the source of her salvation. Prophetically, this follows the time of judgment; individually, the recognition can come at any time to anyone who chooses to trust God. The benefits of seeing God, the Holy One, as the source of salvation are described in these brief chapters.

Praise replaces fear (Isa. 25:1-5). Realizing at last that God is "my God," the believer is moved to

  exalt you and praise your name,
for in perfect faithfulness
  you have done marvelous things,
  things planned long ago.

Isaiah 25:1

The faithfulness of the Savior God is itself a shelter from the storm and a shade from the heat of the coming judgments.

Joy replaces tears (Isa. 25:6-12). The portrait is of a

49

banquet of rich food and aged wine set by God Himself for all peoples. The Sovereign Lord will wipe away all tears, and those who trusted Him will cry out, "Let us rejoice and be glad in his salvation" (25: 9).

Peace replaces oppression (Isa. 26:1-6). The society salvation builds will be righteous, made up of individuals who trust God. Those whose minds are steadfastly fixed on God will have perfect peace, "for the Lord, the Lord, is the Rock eternal" (26: 4).

Righteousness replaces wickedness (Isa. 26:7-11). The redeemed person yearns for God and desires to walk in His ways. This longing for God, rather than the Law, or fear of punishment, is what produces righteousness. The renewed person will want God to be the center of his thoughts and hope.

Humility replaces pride (Isa. 26:12-18). God's people have been haughty and arrogant, but coming to know God has made them see that "you, Lord, establish peace for us; all that we have accomplished you have done for us" (26: 12).

One especially poignant passage describes how redeemed Israel will recognize that she failed to accomplish God's purpose. Rather than being a witness to surrounding lands, Israel chose to follow the pagan ways:

We were with child, we writhed in pain,
  but we gave birth to wind.
We have not brought salvation to the earth;
  we have not given birth to people of the world.
Isaiah 26:18

God will redeem His people. And He Himself will undertake the ministry of world redemption through His Son.

Life replaces death (26:19-21). Because of God, the dead will awake to joy. Isaiah encourages those who know God is their Savior to

> Go, my people, enter your rooms
> and shut the doors behind you;
> hide yourselves for a little while
> until his wrath has passed by.
>
> *Isaiah 26:20*

God is the Savior, but He is also the great Judge. Salvation will come . . . when His wrath has passed by.

The day of wrath (Isa. 27). This section concludes with another sketch of judgment, but without the hints of terror. Through judgment will come blessing: "In that day a great trumpet will sound. Those who were perishing in Assyria and those who were exiled in Egypt will come and worship the Lord on the holy mountain in Jerusalem" (27:13). The revelation of our Savior God brings deliverance.

WOES
Isaiah 28-34

The predominant theme of the first half of Isaiah is one of darkness. Israel has forsaken the way of the Lord and has become, not a light to the nations around her, but *like* the pagan peoples. Her life is

51

made up of arrogance and oppression, war and injustice, terror of enemies within and without.

But not only is the earth dark. Black clouds of judgment are sweeping across the face of the heavens. A warrior, girded for battle, so massive that He seems to block out the very sky, appears. The Holy God, the Sovereign Lord, the great Judge, is about to do battle against arrogance and oppression.

Isaiah cries out a warning, but his people are so committed to wickedness that they do not even glance up! Hearing, they fail to hear. Seeing, they fail to perceive. They respond neither to Isaiah's portraits of judgment nor to his brief, flashing portraits of the glory that will be theirs when the restoring fire has purged the land.

Isaiah then announces that the Holy One is God our Savior; the Judge is the Deliverer. The nation still does not turn to God, but there is some individual response. Some look away from themselves long enough to see God and find in Him the deliverance and peace for which each of us yearns. The individual will have to endure while God works the terror of His judgment. The thunder of battle, the cry of anguish, the last scream of the dying, will echo all around. The isolated person who trusts in God will find security even when

the Lord is coming out of his dwelling
to punish the people of the earth for their sins.
The earth will disclose the blood shed upon her;
she will conceal her slain no more.

Isaiah 26:21

Isaiah has to return to the theme of woe because, while individuals may have responded to his revelation of a Savior God, the nation as a whole did not. They were unwilling to listen to the Lord's instruction and demanded the prophets be silent. They shouted out to Isaiah, "Stop confronting us with the Holy One of Israel"! (30:11) Because the nation rejected God, all the terrors of His judgment will surely come upon them. The woes are pronounced on those who reject salvation's offer.

Woe to Ephraim (Isa. 28). The message to the Northern Kingdom, Ephraim, is to rest in God (v. 12). Unresponsive to the personal dimension of God's message, they had twisted the Word into empty legalism. Stripped of His living presence, the Word of the Lord became

> Do and do, do and do,
> rule on rule, rule on rule;
> a little here, a little there—
> so that they will go and fall backward,
> be injured and snared and captured.
>
> *Isaiah 28:13*

We too can distort Scripture. God's message is not a system of rules to imprison us but a life-style growing from a vital relationship with the living Lord.

Woe to David's city (Isa. 29). God's people are blinded because they have devoted themselves to a life of ritual observances (v. 1). God complains,

These people come near to me with their mouth

and honor me with their lips,
but their hearts are far from me.
Their worship of me
is made up only of rules taught by men.

Isaiah 29:13

How often the revealed faith gets slowly buried as
we interpret and repeat. Soon we lose the reality of
God in the confusing structure of tradition. Then,
beneath all the outward piety, our hearts turn from
God. We devise plans in the darkness and think,
"Who sees us? Who will know?" (v. 15).

How strange that religion itself can so easily rob us
of our sense of God's presence.

Woe to the obstinate nation (Isa. 30). Looking with
love on His straying people, God invites them to
return: "In repentance and rest is your salvation, in
quietness and trust is your strength" (v. 15). But—

They say to the seers,
   "See no more visions"
and to the prophets,
   "Give us no more visions of what is right!
Tell us pleasant things,
   prophesy illusions.
Leave this way,
   get off this path,
and stop confronting us
   with the Holy One of Israel!"

Isaiah 30:10-11

They have stubbornly closed their eyes to Isaiah's

54

vision of God. The Lord longs to be gracious to them (v. 18) and He will answer when they finally cry for help (v. 19). But as long as they reject Him, they will know only woe.

Woe to those who rely on Egypt (Isa. 31). When people have turned from God, in what will they trust? The people of Isaiah's day trusted the military might of their ally, Egypt, and fastened on emptiness.

> The Egyptians are men and not God;
>   their horses are flesh and not spirit.
> When the Lord stretches out his hand,
>   he who helps will stumble,
>   he who is helped will fall;
>   both will perish together.
>
> *Isaiah 31:3*

When we lose sight of God, our perception of reality gets distorted. The fact is that the unseen things are far more real than the seen. Those material things on which we fix our hope when we wander from God are bound to disappoint . . . and to bring woe.

Salvation's certainty (Isa. 32–35). Isaiah affirms that God is Salvation:

> See, a king will reign in righteousness,
>   and rulers will rule with justice.
> He will be like a shelter from the wind,
>   or a refuge from the storm,
> like streams of water in the desert,
>   or the shadow of a great rock in a thirsty land.
>
> *Isaiah 32:1-2*

55

Isaiah details the fruit God's righteousness will produce and reviews the work of the destroyer. He describes the judgments that will finally overthrow the oppressor nations. Then he pictures the joy of the whole world breaking into bloom, as we see the glory and splendor of our God.

Righteousness. Isaiah first focused attention on the corruption and unrighteousness that marked the people's life-style. Now he portrays the righteousness that marks the life-style of the redeemed. When the Spirit of God is poured out on man,

> Justice will dwell in the desert,
>   and righteousness live in the fertile field.
> The fruit of righteousness will be peace;
>   the effect of righteousness will be quietness and
>   confidence forever.

Isaiah 32:16-17

Those who draw upon God's rich store of salvation can live in the presence of the consuming fire. Who can reside with the Holy One?

> He who lives righteously
>   and speaks what is right,
> who rejects gain from extortion
>   and keeps his hand from accepting bribes,
> who stops his ears against plots of murder
>   and shuts his eyes against contemplating evil—
> this is the man who will dwell in the heights.

Isaiah 33:15-16

GOING DEEPER

to personalize

1. Read quickly through chapters 25—35 and underline anything that describes the relationship God seeks to develop with His people. What does God desire in His relationship with you?

2. Select from Isaiah 25—35 two chapters that you would like to explore more carefully. For each decide:

- What is the main teaching?
- What is the most important verse to you?
- What is a significant application for believers today?

2. Choose one or more of the following to memorize:

- Isa. 25:1
- Isa. 29:13
- Isa. 33:5-6
- Isa. 25:9
- Isa. 30:15
- Isa. 33:15-16
- Isa. 26:3-4
- Isa. 32:1-2
- Isa. 35:3-4

to probe

What can you find in Scripture about God as Savior or Deliverer? Use a concordance and focus on the Old Testament revelation.

Interlude
A VISIT TO HISTORY
Isaiah 36—39

5

THE TURNING POINT

DO NOT LET HEZEKIAH mislead you when he says, 'The Lord will deliver us.' Has the god of any nation ever delivered his land from the hand of the king of Assyria? Where are the gods of Hamath and Arpad? Where are the gods of Sepharvaim? Have they rescued Samaria from my hand? Who of all the gods of these countries has been able to save his land from me? So how can the Lord deliver Jerusalem from my hand?

Isaiah 36:18-19

Isaiah interrupts his prophecies for a historical interlude. Uzziah, Jotham, and Ahaz have died. The predictions Isaiah made in their time about Syria and the Northern Kingdom have come to pass. Just as Isaiah warned, Assyria has mercilessly swept into the Middle East, crushing all enemies, and the men and women of the Northern Kingdom have been deported following a bitter three-year siege. By 722

B.C. the Kingdom of Israel was no more. Later, in 711 B.C., another coalition was formed by the subject peoples. These allies, who included Egypt, were defeated by Sargon. Possibly due to Isaiah's warnings (20: 1-6), Judah did not join the rebels and was spared for a time. Laird Harris describes the intervening years:

Sennacherib, Sargon's son (705-681) invaded Judah, who had on several occasions before paid tribute to Assyria. Tiglath-pileser III claimed tribute from "Azariah of Yaudi" (Judah) and "Jehoahaz (Ahaz) of Judah." Second Kings 16: 8 mentions tribute paid by Ahaz to Tiglath-pileser III, and it is probable that Sargon also received tribute. Hezekiah gave to Sennacherib 300 talents of silver and thirty talents of gold (2 Kings 18: 14). The Philistine area had rebelled with Egyptian help, and bound Padi, the Assyrian puppet, at Ekron and sent him to Hezekiah. Sennacherib overcame the Egyptians and the coalition in the battle of Eltekeh about 701 B.C. He conquered forty-six cities of Judah, took 200,150 captives, resettled Padi in Ekron, and received Hezekiah's submission. He claimed thirty talents of gold, 800 talents of silver, which may be a more inclusive reckoning than 2 Kings 18: 14 (or, more likely, a mere exaggeration), and much other plunder. Judah was brought low. Significantly, Sennacherib said he besieged Jerusalem and Hezekiah "like a caged bird shut up in Jerusalem his royal city," but does not claim that he conquered the city. The Bible makes it clear that Jerusalem was spared.[1]

The year, then, is about 700 B.C. Isaiah the

prophet has ministered in Judah for some forty years. He has seen many of his words fulfilled in his own time . . . and has seen the evil Ahaz replaced on the throne by his son Hezekiah, who was one of Judah's most godly kings: "He did what was right in the eyes of the Lord, according to all that David his ancestor had done" (2 Chronicles 29: 2). As soon as he ascended the throne at age twenty-five, he reopened the Temple, which his father had closed. He reassembled the priests and Levites and exhorted his people to return to God. He publicly exhorted these men, whom Mosaic Law set apart to lead in worship:

Now it is in my heart to make a covenant with the Lord, the God of Israel, that his fierce anger may turn away from us. My sons, do not now be negligent, for the Lord has chosen you to stand in his presence, to minister to him, and to be his ministers and burn incense to him.

2 Chronicles 29:10-11

Having suddenly and decisively reinstituted Temple worship and sacrifice, the king sent messengers throughout Judah exhorting the people to turn to God. He invited all to come to Jerusalem for the Passover feast, which had not been kept for centuries.

The king's messengers cried throughout the land:

Do not now be stiff-necked as your fathers were, but yield yourself to the Lord, and come to his sanctuary, which he has sanctified for ever, and serve the Lord your God, that his fierce anger may turn away from you. For if you return to the Lord, your brethren and your children will find compassion with their captors, and return to this land. For the Lord your God is gracious and merciful, and will not turn away his face from you, if you return to him.

2 Chronicles 30: 8-9

Hezekiah showed a total commitment to God. The Bible tells us that "all he did was good and right and faithful before the Lord his God" (2 Chron. 31: 20). And the land prospered.

Invasion. In Hezekiah's fourteenth year his faith was put to the test. Sennacherib of Assyria invaded Judah and captured the fortified cities that had been built to ring the land. Even Lachish, supposed impregnable, had fallen.

The Assyrian ruler sent his army field commander and several other officials to demand Jerusalem's surrender. Strikingly, this delegation met Hezekiah's envoys "at the aqueduct of the Upper Pool, on the road to the Washerman's Field" (Isa. 36: 2). This was the place where Ahaz had been confronted by Isaiah years before and had been promised that he need not fear Rezin and Pekah (7: 3). Ahaz, the godless king of Judah, had sneered at the Lord's promises and had put his faith in alliances. Now his son, faced with even more imminent danger, placed his faith in God, the *only* hope of His people.

There on that spot the field commander demanded surrender and sneered at the strange confidence Hezekiah continued to display. After all, Assyria had already pummeled Judah's outer defenses. "On what are you basing this confidence of yours?" the commander snapped. Egypt? A mere nothing! "And if you say to me, 'We are depending on the Lord our God'—isn't he the one whose high places and altars Hezekiah removed, saying to Judah and Jerusalem, 'You must worship before this altar'?" (36: 4-7)

The Assyrians saw Hezekiah's purification of the land only as an attack on the god of the region. But even if they had understood Hezekiah's reasons, they would have sneered. What's the difference between one god and another? Crying out in Hebrew, in a voice loud enough for the people of Judah watching from the city walls to hear, the Assyrian commander issued his challenge. "Who of all the gods of these countries has been able to save his land from me? So how can the Lord deliver Jerusalem from my hand?" (36: 20). The Assyrians recognized no difference between the idols of the nations they had destroyed and the living God of Judah. In their apostasy Israel and Judah had lost far more than their own blessing. They had lost their opportunity to reveal God as the God of all men.

Israel's mission. It is important not to miss the evangelistic mission of Israel in the Old Testament. We catch a glimpse of this purpose in the original Covenant with Abraham: "By you all the families of the earth shall be blessed" (Gen. 12: 3). In the

Exodus the mighty acts were designed as a demonstration for Egypt as well as Israel, that "the Egyptians may know that I am the Lord" (Exod. 7:5). Rahab of Jericho found a refuge for herself in the God of Israel when she helped the spies. She reported on the morale of Jericho: "Our hearts melted ... for the Lord your God is he who is God in heaven above and on earth beneath" (Jos. 2:11).

Again and again as Israel lived in harmony with God, the Lord revealed Himself through her. While many trembled in fear at that revelation, a few, like Rahab, placed their trust in the God of Israel.

The holy life-style of Israel as well as her military strength was to be a living testimony that would draw others to know and worship God. Moses told the people just before they entered Canaan:

> Keep [these statutes and ordinances] and do them; for that will be your wisdom and your understanding in the sight of the peoples, who, when they hear all these statutes, will say, "Surely this great nation is a wise and understanding people." For what great nation is there that has a god so near to it as the Lord our God is to us, whenever we call upon him? And what great nation is there, that has statutes and ordinances so righteous as all this law which I set before you this day?
>
> *Deuteronomy 4:6-8*

As Israel lived a holy life, close to God, they could be sure He would intervene on their behalf in such a way that other nations could come to know Him.

How tragic, then, to realize that when a later generation recognized God as its salvation, it had to look back over wasted years of history and admit,

> We were with child, we writhed in pain,
> but we gave birth to wind.
> We have not brought salvation to the earth;
> we have not given birth to people of the world.
>
> *Isaiah 16:18*

But there were times when the opportunity came to reveal God . . . and the people responded. This moment of trial under Hezekiah was one such opportunity.

Dependence. When Hezekiah heard the Assyrian's challenge, he immediately humbled himself (represented by the tearing of his clothes and choosing sackcloth for dress). He hurried to the Temple and spread out before the Lord the letter of ridicule. Hezekiah knew God was alive, present with him, and able to deliver His people. He prayed,

> O Lord Almighty, God of Israel, enthroned between the cherubim, you alone are God over all the kingdoms of the earth. You have made heaven and earth. Give ear, O Lord, and hear; open your eyes, O Lord, and see; listen to all the words Sennacherib has sent to insult the living God. . . . Now, O Lord our God, deliver us from his hand, so that all kingdoms on earth may know that you alone, O Lord, are God.
>
> *Isaiah 37:16-17, 20*

In response to Hezekiah's prayer, Isaiah was sent with God's promise: Within three years the land Sennacherib has devasted will be restored to fruitfulness. And as far as Jerusalem is concerned, not an arrow will fly over its wall.

> I will defend this city and save it,
>> for my sake and for the sake of David my servant.

Isaiah 37:35

That night 185,000 men of the Assyrian army died in their sleep. Immediately Sennacherib broke camp and returned to Nineveh, his capital. Not one Assyrian arrow had flown over the walls of the Holy City.

REVELATION

In the first half of Isaiah (chapters 1—35), the prophet emphasizes a portrait of God Himself. If only Israel can *see God*, her whole way of life and her circumstances will radically change. She will reject wickedness in favor of righteousness. She will know peace rather than warfare and the terror of surrounding enemies. The Living God of Israel will act both *in* her and *for* her.

The historical interlude of chapters 36—39 demonstrates this theme beautifully. Hezekiah is a king who *does* see God! How clear is his vision: "O Lord Almighty, God of Israel, enthroned between the cherubim, you alone are God over all the kingdoms of the earth. You have made heaven and earth . . .

you alone, O Lord, are God" (37: 16, 20). Hezekiah keeps his priorities straight as he responds to God. He first purifies his own land, restores the worship of God, and seeks to establish justice. Then when enemy nations invade, there is no frantic appeal for alliance with the powers of this world. Instead, he calls on the God of heaven to act. And God does.

If only Israel had maintained her clear vision of who God is, how different her behavior would have been. And how different her fate! To see clearly who God is, is always a necessary foundation for faith.

The second part of Isaiah (chapters 40—66) emphasizes the purposes to which God has committed Himself. The final and complete fulfillment of God's good plan for mankind captures the prophet's imagination and fills his view.

Noting these two emphases helps us understand much about the structure of Isaiah and the structure and purpose of the entire Old Testament. Through His Word, God invites us to know Him *and* to know his purposes so that we might grow in faith and trust.

It's clear, as we read Isaiah, that these emphases are not limited to one section of the book. The first half gives us flashes of insight into God's ultimate plans. And the second half adds dramatically to our understanding of God's character. But in general the thrust does differ along these lines. Chapters 1—35 confront us with vivid portraits of God, particularly as His character is known in the actions He will take in history. Chapters 40—66 give vital expositions of God's purposes, particularly as they relate to His ultimate plans for His children.

Looking back, we can recall similar divisions in Genesis. In the early chapters (1—11) we saw initial affirmation that we live in a *personal universe.* Behind the physical universe is a living being, and He is the ultimate reality. Then, in the rest of Genesis (12—50), we discovered that we live in a *purposive universe.* In the Covenant made with Abraham, God indicates that history has direction and a goal. God has a purpose for man that He *will* fulfill; He has committed Himself to it. So it is particularly appropriate to begin our Old Testament studies with Genesis (where these twin themes are introduced) and to end them in Isaiah (where they have their fullest development). Throughout history, in Word and deed, God has provided a progressive revelation of *Himself* and of His *intentions.* We began our studies in Genesis with just a glimpse of God's character and plans for man. Now in Isaiah comes a much fuller unveiling.

Why the interlude? Even when we see the difference in focus of the two halves of the Book of Isaiah, we may wonder about the reason for the historic interlude. What is its role here?

In a very basic way, the story of Hezekiah's confrontation with Sennacherib helps us grasp the impact the Word of God can have on human experience. We also see the way He reveals His Word to those who do not believe.

First, it was only because Hezekiah had a clear vision of who God is that he dared to resist Assyria. It

GOD'S REVELATION GOALS

	GENESIS	ISAIAH
God reveals Himself	a personal universe (1-11)	here is the Person! (1-35)
God reveals His plan	a covenant promise (12-50)	here the fulfillment is described (40-66)

was only because Hezekiah was sure that God has committed Himself to do good for His people that he turned to God with expectation. *It is only as you and I fix our eyes on the living God, as we believe that His plans are for our welfare, that we find freedom in our "now" to act in faith.* Hezekiah knew the God of Scripture was trustworthy, and he shows us how to live out our trust in Him.

Indeed, this is the purpose for which His Word was revealed: that in knowing and trusting Him we might respond to His self-revelation, and in responding our present experience might be changed.

How does God acting in our lives communicate the reality of God to nonbelievers? In this way. Although they may reject written revelation's portrait of God and his purposes, they cannot deny events in space and time. The deliverance of Judah was a mute testimony to Assyria that the Lord God of Israel is *not* like other gods. Assyria chose to reject that testimony, as the Northern Kingdom, Israel,

71

had rejected the testimony of the written Word. *But nevertheless, God revealed Himself in space and time through His acts on behalf of His people.*

Many will reject every testimony to God. But among the many will always be a Rahab . . . a person who looks beyond space/time events and sees God, not as some nameless terror, but as a Person reaching out with love.

And so it is today as well.

As you and I see in the Word of God an ever clearer picture of the Person we worship, our daily choices will be affected. Trusting Him frees us to obey. As we respond in obedience, God makes Himself known in the circumstances of our lives.

GOING DEEPER
to personalize

1. Read the historical background of this period. This includes Isaiah 36—39 and 2 Chronicles 29—32.

2. What do you make of the story in Isaiah 39 and the commentary on it in 2 Chronicles 32? Did Hezekiah fulfill God's revealed purpose for him in this situation, or not? And what difference would that make?

3. Skimming through Isaiah 1—35, what indications can you find that God has always intended to reveal Himself *through* His people as well as *to* them?

4. List at least five "Lessons for life today" that you might draw from Isaiah 36—39 and 2 Chronicles 20—32.

to probe

1. How many passages in the Old Testament can you find that indicate an evangelistic purpose for Israel among the surrounding nations?

2. Find at least three Old Testament personalities who chose to believe God as Hezekiah did in this crisis. Then locate and compare at least three who in similar crises made different choices. In each case, what was the outcome for the individual, for God's people as a whole, and for the Gentile observers?

1. R. L. Harris, *Zondervan Pictorial Encyclopedia of the Bible*, 5 vols. (Grand Rapids: Zondervan, 1976), 3:314.

6

HIS NAME IS WONDERFUL

"FOR UNTO US a child is born
  to us a son is given,
and the government will be upon his shoulders.
And he will be named
  Wonderful Counselor, Mighty God,
Everlasting Father, Prince of Peace.

Isaiah 9:6

How carefully the prophet used words! Looking back from the perspective of the New Testament, it is so clear. "Unto us a *child* is born." When God entered the world in the person of Jesus, He came as a human being, experienced the same kind of birth as you and I. He grew, matured, became a man . . . all within the framework of natural process. A child was born.

But then the prophet adds, "To us a *son* is given." The child born was the very Son of God, whose natural birth was preceded by a supernatural conception. God and man linked forever, welded eternally to be one, the natural and supernatural bonded together in incarnation. And then the prophet explains: "He will be named Wonderful Counselor, Mighty God, Everlasting Father, Prince of Peace."

The names alert us that the child born will be God's gift of His divine Son.

NAMES

In our Western culture names point to the individual. They are designations. John Q. Smith is a different person than John B. Smith, but for neither individual is his "Smithness" of particular significance.

It's different in many cultures. The names of native Americans were often chosen to reflect something distinctive about the person or the events surrounding his or her birth. "Falling Star" might reflect the first sight a girl's father saw as he glanced toward the sky after her birth. "He Who Hunts Eagles" might mark out a man with pride; "Big Belly" might be a lifelong mark of derision.

In many cultures, particularly the Semitic peoples of Scripture, names have meaning; they describe the person. For instance, the Book of Judges tells us that after Gideon had been God's instrument to save Israel from the Midianites, the people came and asked Gideon to be king. "Rule over us," they said, "you and your son and your grandson also" (8: 22). Gideon rejected this invitation to establish a hereditary monarchy. But later the same passage tells us of the birth of a son whom Gideon names. And what does the name mean? It is a construction of the Hebrew words *abv* ("father") with the suffix *i* ("my") and *melech* ("king"). Abimelech literally means "my father is king"!

In that name we see Gideon falling away from his early resolve. We also see the seeds of future events. Judges 9 goes on to describe how after the death of Gideon this same Abimelech killed all his brothers and attempted to set himself up as king—before he himself was killed. His name revealed the desire of his father and, perhaps, set the course Abimelech chose to follow.

Old Testament names, in a sense, almost take part in the reality of who the people are. It's easy to see, then, why the commandment says, "You shall not take the name of the Lord your God in vain; for the Lord will not hold him guiltless who takes his name in vain" (Exod. 20: 7). All too often we have translated this mandate as "You shall not swear." But it is far more than this. God's names are instruments of revelation. They tell us something of Him in His essential person. To take a name in vain means literally to count it an empty thing. This commandment warns us that when God reveals Himself to us as the Holy One of Israel, we are not to take His holiness lightly. When God calls Himself the Sovereign Lord, we are not to ignore His sovereign power over all nations and, like Ahaz, dash to make alliances with some neighboring king. *We are to take the names of God seriously, because they are means of God's self-disclosure.* In the names of God, we meet the person of the Lord Himself.

This understanding of names also underlies such New Testament promises of Jesus as "I will do whatever you ask in My name" (John 14:13). This promise is not an invitation to ritually tack on "in Jesus' name" to our prayers. It is instead the promise that as we pray in harmony with who Jesus is—with His character and purposes—God will respond with a resounding "Amen."

How vital, then, to examine carefully the names God bears, and thru them to grasp more and more of Him. How vital that we treat God's names not as a fraudulent or flippant expression, but as a significant communication to us of the very essence of His person. As we meditate on a name, we not only know God better, but we are able to conform our own lives to His.

PRIMARY OLD TESTAMENT NAMES

God. The basic term for God in the Semitic world is *El.* It is one of the oldest designations and is often combined with other words to make compound descriptions, such as *El Shaddai,* "God Almighty." This general and inclusive name seems to signify power or ability, particularly the great transcendent power that stands outside and behind nature. (God's power might be shown in the thunderstorm—but the thunderstorm is not God.)

Lord. This term occurs frequently in the earlier history of Israel. It is rooted in the word *adon* and *adonai.* While *El* was used by all the Semitic peoples, *adonai* was used mainly by the Hebrews.

When this word is used of human beings, it refers to those who have authority. For instance, it might be used by a woman of her husband, or a courtier might address the king, "O my lord the king. . . ."

This name stresses that God is over all things; to Him we owe obedience and loyalty. Its usage shows clearly the Old Testament recognized God as no mere local deity but as God who is Lord over the whole earth (see Josh. 3:11).

Yahweh. This is the third and undoubtedly most significant of the three basic Old Testament names of God. It was only to the Hebrew people, and to no other nation, that God revealed this name. The Jews recognized the specialness of *Yahweh* (which is the proper form for the mistranslated English name *Jehovah).* In later times scribes who wrote the name as they copied Scripture immediately took a purifying bath. The name was so holy that it was not spoken aloud in later times but referred to only as "the Name." More than any other name, it communicates the unique and special relationship God establishes with His own people.

What, then, is the significance of *Yahweh?*

We glimpse its meaning first in Exodus. Moses was called from the wilderness to go to Pharaoh's court as God's instrument of deliverance for Israel:

> Then Moses said to God, "I am to go, then, to the sons of Israel and say to them, 'The God of your fathers has sent me to you.' But if they ask me

what his name is, what am I to tell them?" And God said to Moses, "I Am who I Am. This," he added, "is what you must say to the sons of Israel: 'I Am has sent me to you.' " And God also said to Moses, "You are to say to the sons of Israel: 'Yahweh, the God of your fathers, the God of Abraham, the God of Isaac, and the God of Jacob, has sent me to you.' This is my name for all time; by this name I shall be invoked for all generations to come."

Exodus 3:13-15, Jerusalem Bible

Later, in Egypt, God speaks again to Moses about His name. "I am Yahweh. To Abraham and Isaac and Jacob I appeared as El Shaddai; I did not make myself known to them by my name Yahweh" (Exod. 6: 2-3, Jerusalem Bible). Now, through Moses, God was going to provide a demonstration of Himself as Yahweh, and by that name He is to be remembered by His people forever.

What, then, does *Yahweh* mean? The name is formed of four consonants, JHWH. Because these consonants are a form of the Hebrew verb "to be," some versions translate their first appearance in Exodus as "I AM." But far more than God's existence is implied. While *Yahweh* does mean "the God Who Is," its implications are better understood as *"the God Who Is Always Present."*

While the patriarchs knew the name *Yahweh*, they used it infrequently and did not grasp its full meaning. Now, in Moses' time, Israel would feel the full impact of the fact that God is the One Who Is Present. God, through Moses, broke dramatically into space and time. In a series of mighty acts of devastation God freed His people and led them out of Egypt. God acted to destroy the pursuing army at the Red (or Reed) Sea. God provided daily manna to feed them. God guided them in the fiery pillar of cloud that went before them in the years of wilderness wandering. In unmistakable ways God proved to His people that He was present with them and that in His presence was their assurance of deliverance. It was in His character as Yahweh, the One Who Is Ever Present with His people, that God chose to be remembered throughout all generations. Israel was never to forget that God had committed Himself to them: to walk beside them, to support, to strengthen, to sanctify, and to save.

FORGOTTEN

But Israel did forget. The tragic history of so many empty years demonstrates that to generation after generation God became a mere tradition. He was little more than a memory associated with Abraham or Moses . . . a hope for a better tomorrow . . . but still not a God of *today*.

It's so easy for us as well to push God off into the past or future. We honestly rejoice in the historic death and resurrection of Jesus. We honestly yearn for His return. But we fail to remember God the way He Himself has chosen to be remembered throughout *all* generations. God wants us to know Him as Yahweh, the Person Who Is Present with us *now*.

This is the great cry of Isaiah! He called to a nation that, in spite of several godly kings, still failed to remember that God is present. Sensing His holy presence, how can we turn as a nation to sin and injustice?

God is with us as Sovereign Lord, Isaiah reminds. How then can His people quake in terror at the military might of Syria or Assyria? They are mere men, and God, the Sovereign Lord Himself, is present with us!

God is present with us as Judge. How quickly then we must judge our own sins and turn to Him. How surely He will act to judge the sin that mars our lives, and how surely He will act to judge the enemy who works injustice on us.

God is present with us as Savior. How much peace and joy this realization brings. Forgiven, restored, we stand again on Mount Zion, awaiting the promised festival.

> We have a strong city;
>   God makes salvation
>   its walls and ramparts.
> Open the gates
>   that the righteous nation may enter,
>   the nation that keeps faith.
> You will keep in perfect peace
>   him whose mind is steadfast,
>   because he trusts in you.
> Trust in the Lord forever,
>   for the Lord, the Lord, is the Rock Eternal.
> *Isaiah 26:1-4*

81

We may not see that city raised in our time. But the Lord we have with us *now* is the Rock Eternal on which it rests. In Him we have the present experience of the perfect peace salvation promises.

SECONDARY NAMES OF GOD

What are some other names for God? Rock. Highest. Holy One. Mighty One. Light-Giver. Counselor. Judge. Father. Redeemer. Savior. Deliverer. Shield. Strength. Almighty. Righteous One. Lord of Armies. On and on they range in wonderful display. And each one reveals *Him.* Each opens our eyes to another aspect of His wonder. Each holds out for us another dimension of promise. Meeting God in His revealed names, we cry out with Isaiah,

> Surely this is our God;
>   we trusted in him, and he saved us.
> This is the Lord, we trust in him;
>   let us rejoice and be glad in his salvation.
>
> *Isaiah 25:9*

GOING DEEPER
to personalize

This week's *personalize* suggestions will lead you to explore one or more names of God and their meaning. As you read through the selected portions, you'll want to be aware of a particular fact. We noted that *Adonai* means "Lord" and is translated that way.

But in our English translations *Yahweh* is also translated "Lord," not "Yahweh" or "I AM" or "The One Always Present." How can you tell when you read whether the Hebrew text reads *Adonai* or *Yahweh?*

The translators chose to use a capital first letter and three lower-case letters ("Lord") when the original text indicates *Adonai.* But when the original text indicates *Yahweh,* the English reads "LORD."

1. Select any three chapters from either the first or second half of Isaiah. What names of God are given in these chapters? What would the names communicate to Judah? What do the names communicate about God to you?

2. Select one of the often-repeated names of God in Isaiah. Study the occurrences of this name in either the first or second half of Isaiah (1—35 or 40—66). Write out a summary of what this name communicated to Judah, and how God, as He revealed Himself through this name, affected life then. How can God in that expression of His character affect *your* life?

3. Use a concordance to see how many different Old Testament names of God you can locate. (Often names are linked to "God" or "Lord," such as "Lord of Hosts." So begin your concordance search with *G* and *L.*) List all the names you can find and venture a one-sentence suggestion of what that name might mean to God's people.

to probe

1. Several books have been written on names of God. Locate, read, and report on one.

2. Choose one name of God and meditate on it for several days. Write a report or journal on how that fresh awareness of Him has affected *your* today.

Part Two

VISIONS OF SPLENDOR
Isaiah 40—66

THE EVERLASTING GOD

THIS IS WHAT the Lord says—
 Israel's king and Redeemer, the Lord
  Almighty:
I am the first and I am the last;
 apart from me there is no God.
Who then is like me? Let him proclaim it.
 Let him declare and lay out before me
what has happened since I established my ancient
  people,
 and what is yet to come—
 yes, let him foretell what will come.
Do not tremble, do not be afraid.
 Did I not proclaim this and foretell it long ago?
You are my witnesses. Is there any God besides
  me?
 No, there is no other Rock; I know not one.
                              Isaiah 44:6-8

With this chapter we move into the second half of
Isaiah and immediately burst into a fresh and joyful
world. A tone of optimism and celebration pervades
these last chapters of the prophet's work. We hear

that tone in the very first words of Isaiah 40:

> Comfort, comfort my people,
>   says your God.
> Speak tenderly to Jerusalem,
>   and proclaim to her
> that her hard service has been completed,
>   that her sin has been paid for,
> that she has received from the Lord's hand
>   double for all her sins.
>
> *Isaiah 40:1-2*

In this half of Isaiah the prophet seems to *look back* on judgment past. The prospect of terror is gone. Now comes the promised joy. Isaiah looks beyond even the Babylonian Captivity of Judah, still a hundred years in his future, and sees Babylon's power destroyed by Cyrus of Persia (Isa. 45—46). He looks beyond even this, to the restoration of all things. In prophetic vision Isaiah sees history's end, when God will say to his redeemed people,

> Forget the former things;
>   do not dwell on the past.
> See, I am doing a new thing!
>   Now it springs up; do you not perceive it?
> I am making a way in the desert
>   and streams in the wasteland. . . .
> to give drink to my people, my chosen,
>   the people I formed for myself
> that they may recount my praise.
>
> *Isaiah 43:18-19, 21*

In the new world, former things will not be remembered or come to mind. God will make all things new.

PIVOTAL THEMES

Isaiah's looking back at terrible judgment from the perspective of the joyful experience of God's promised blessing brings two pivotal themes into focus.

Theme 1: Scripture as revelation. In the last chapter we saw that one dramatic means through which God reveals Himself to His people is through His *names.*

But there came a point in time when God also revealed Himself in man's language! God communicated Himself to us through words spoken by prophets and recorded in written form in the Scriptures. Through the written word, we too are invited to know and trust God.

We can watch an individual's actions. We can draw conclusions about him from what we observe. But we can never know his motives or his feelings, what is in his heart, unless he explains himself to us in words.

The Apostle Paul makes this point in 1 Corinthians. "For who among men knows the thoughts of a man except the man's spirit within him? In the same way no one knows the thoughts of God except the Spirit of God." Paul goes on to point out that in the Bible we have "words not taught us by human wisdom but in words taught by the Spirit" (1 Cor. 2:11, 13). Scripture is far more than the record of man's groping after God. It is more than human theories of the meaning of history. The Bible, as prophet after prophet has proclaimed, is the recorded Word of God. It is His revelation, through which we come to know Him as He shares His inmost thoughts with us!

Isaiah 40—48 presents one particular aspect of God's inmost thoughts: His intentions. We are given a unique insight into God's Person as we read these words about His plans for man's better tomorrow:

> I the Lord will answer them;
> I, the God of Israel, will not forsake them.
> I will make the rivers flow on barren heights,
> and springs within the valleys.
> I will turn the desert into pools of water,
> and the parched ground into springs.
> I will put in the desert
> the cedar and acacia, the myrtle and the olive.
>
> *Isaiah 41:17-19*

God intends to restore the shattered land and the shattered people, so He may bring a celebrating people back to Himself.

We do not study the Bible just to gain information. We come to Scripture to meet God. *If we truly want to know God, you and I must look into the Word of God and listen to Him share what is in His heart. We must look beyond the darkness of our todays to catch a vision of the bright sunshine of God's promised tomorrow.*

How can we be sure it's really Him we see in Scripture, and not some dream or weird vision drawn from overactive imaginations? This was a problem for Israel as well as for modern man to which God gave a distinct answer. He challenged Judah concerning the idols on which she had fixed her hope:

> Bring in your idols to tell us
>> what is going to happen. . . .
> declare to us the things to come,
>> tell us what the future holds,
> so we may know that you are gods.
>> *Isaiah 41:22-23*

Then God established His own unique claim:

> I foretold the former things long ago,
>> my mouth announced them and I made them known. . . .
> I told you these things long ago;
>> before they happened I announced them to you
> so that you could not say,
>> 'My idols did them. . . .'
> From now on I will tell you of new things,
>> of hidden things unknown to you.
>> *Isaiah 48:3, 5-6*

God announced through the prophets what would happen in Israel's history; invariably His words came true. God has verified the trustworthiness of His revelation through fulfilled prophecy. Just how accurate prophecy has proven to be was considered in another book of this series, *Springtime Coming*. And we'll see again the trustworthiness of the spoken Word as we look (in chapter 9) at Jehovah's Servant and see history work out prophecy concerning Him in minutest detail. For now we simply want to note that the Old and New Testaments alike speak with sure conviction that the words recorded are God's. They accurately reveal Him. Prophecy not only vindicates God's claim of self-revelation; it moves the expression of God's good intentions for mankind beyond *possibility* to *certainty*. In Scripture's statement of God's plans, we meet *Him,* and we read history before it happens!

Theme 2: God as ever living. How can we be sure that what is portrayed by Isaiah as future history will come to pass? He has an answer for us in God's revelation of Himself as everlasting. He Himself will be present in the future to keep the wondrous promises He gives.

But Israel and Judah have turned aside from the living God to follow *idols!* Isaiah in these last chapters contrasts the power of God with the ineffectiveness of idols:

> To whom then will you compare God?
> What image will you compare him to?
> As for an idol, a craftsman casts it,
> and a goldsmith overlays it with gold
> and fashions silver chains for it.
> A man too poor to present such an offering
> selects wood that will not rot.
> He looks for a skilled craftsman,
> to set up an idol that will not topple.
> *Isaiah 40:19-20*

But God is no idol that must be nailed down so it won't topple (41:7). God sits enthroned above the earth. He looks down and sees mankind as we see grasshoppers, insignificant below Him (40:22).
How foolish the idol maker. He cuts down a tree, uses some of it to build a fire and cook his food, and then he makes an idol from the rest.

He . . . fashions a god and worships it;
   he makes an idol and bows down to it.
Half of it he burns in the fire; . . .
From the rest he makes a god, his idol; . . .
He prays to it and says,
   "Save me; you are my god."

Isaiah 44:15-17

Unbelievable! To bow down to a block of wood! And to choose such gods when the Living God, the Maker of Heaven and Earth, presents Himself to us to be known and worshiped, to be our Healer and Redeemer. The Lord says,

Before me no god was formed,
   nor will there be one after me.
I, even I am the Lord,
   and apart from me there is no savior.
I have revealed and redeemed and
   proclaimed. . . .

Isaiah 43:10-12

I have revealed. I have redeemed. I have proclaimed.

93

It is the Living God who has revealed Himself to us in His Word. On Him Isaiah bases all his hope and his confidence. A vision of the Everlasting God dominates Isaiah's thoughts. The Everlasting God, the First and Last, the Living One, whom we meet in Isaiah 40—48, is the one on whom all our hopes must rest.

PURPOSES OF THE LIVING GOD
Isaiah 40-48

In these opening chapters we are shown God's intentions and reassured that what He intends will come to pass.

> I am God, and there is no other;
> I am God, and there is none like me.
> I make known the end from the beginning,
>   from ancient times what is still to come.
> I say: My purpose will stand,
>   and I will do all that I please.
>
> *Isaiah 46:9-10*

What, then, does God please to do?
* *Comfort: Isaiah 40.* In this chapter God is seen coming with power. But not to judge! Instead

> He tends his flock like a shepherd:
>   He gathers the lambs in his arms
> and carries them close to his heart;
>   he gently leads those that have young.
>
> *Isaiah 40:11*

He who will never grow weary or tired is now seen giving strength to weary people, renewing their strength. God's intentions for us are good; He cares for His sheep.

● *Help: Isaiah 41.* The idols in which Israel and Judah trusted are vain things. But God Himself will lead His people to a time of rejoicing:

> I will strengthen you and help you;
> I will uphold you with my righteous right
>   hand. . . .
> For I am the Lord your God,
>   who takes hold of your right hand
> and says to you, Do not fear;
>   I will help you.
>
> *Isaiah 41:10, 13*

● *Fully restore: Isaiah 42–43.* In these chapters God contrasts the past and the future. When all the former things have been put behind, there will be a new song of praise for God's people to sing. Then the Lord Himself, apart from whom there is no savior, will be their redeemer, bringing them forgiveness and joy.

> Yes, and from ancient days I am he.
> No one can deliver out of my hand.
> When I act, who can reverse it?
>
> *Isaiah 43:13*

● *To be forever: Isaiah 44.* God commits Himself to restore Jerusalem and stand forever as Israel's King.

95

In this chapter is the most devastating critique of idolatry in all of Scripture. Because our God is no empty man-made idol, we can even now

> Sing for joy, O heavens, for the Lord has done this;
> shout aloud, O earth beneath.
> Burst out into song, you mountains,
> you forests and all your trees.
> For the Lord has redeemed Jacob,
> he displays his glory in Israel.
>
> *Isaiah 44:23*

● *To destroy Babylon: Isaiah 45–47.* Looking beyond the current Assyrian danger, the prophet foresees the end of another nation, Babylon. It would be another hundred years before Babylon would carry Judah away captive even as Sargon had carried away Israel.

For unaided men, this kind of prophecy seems impossible. In fact, scholars who discuss the possibility of propositional revelation have been sure that some man other than Isaiah must have written the latter half of his book. But God reminds us in these very chapters,

> I foretold the former things long ago,
> my mouth announced them and I made them known;
> then suddenly I acted, and they came to pass.
>
> *Isaiah 48:3*

The Bible presents God as the Living God, the Everlasting One, who not only announces the future but who acts to bring about foretold events. If we accept the possibility of a living God, as opposed to a mere expression of man's imagination or need, then there is nothing terribly unlikely about the prophet looking *back* on a day that is still future to his own time. After all, it is God who speaks through him. And God, the Living God Who Is Always Present with His people, is in a unique position to *know*.

The Living God speaks to us now and, in His promise of restoration, reveals Himself to us as a God of endless love.

GOING DEEPER

to personalize

1. Skim chapters 40—48 of Isaiah. What intentions (statements of what God says He will do) can you find? What do these statements tell you about Him as a person?

2. From your study above, write a one-page personality sketch of God.

3. Read the classic chapter (Isa. 44) discussing the folly of idolatry, and answer these questions:

   (a) What are some modern idols?
   (b) What is the contrast between modern idols and the Living God?
   (c) What is the most important thing God seems to want to get across to us in this chapter?

4. Here are some special passages from these chapters to memorize:

- Isa. 40:11
- Isa. 40:28-31
- Isa. 41:13

- Isa. 43:1-2
- Isa. 46:9-10

to probe

1. What can you find out about idolatry? How did it affect the life of God's Old Testament people?

2. What is the relationship between propositional revelation (concepts, ideas, information about God) and person revelation (God's self-disclosure)? Check out this relationship in several theology texts, and write a report.

THE SERVANT

AND NOW the Lord says—
  he who formed me in the womb to be his servant
to bring Jacob back to him
  and gather Israel again to himself,
for I am honored in the eyes of the Lord
  and my God has been my strength—
he says:
"It is too small a thing for you to be my servant
  to restore the tribes of Jacob
  and bring back those of Israel I have kept.
I will also make you a light for the Gentiles,
  that you may bring my salvation to the ends of
    the earth."

This is what the Lord says—
  the Redeemer and Holy One of Israel—
to him who was despised and abhorred by the
    nation,

to the servant of rulers:
"Kings will see you and arise,
    princes will see and bow down,
because of the Lord, who is faithful."

Isaiah 49:5-7

A servant?

At first the title "Servant" seems out of place among all the splendorous titles Isaiah gives God: The Holy One. The Redeemer. The Sovereign God. The Everlasting God. All these names seem so much more appropriate to that person who is unveiled in this great prophetic book. Yet "Servant" may most fully reveal the glory and the wonder of our God.

Certainly the title is one that Jesus often chose for Himself. He held out his own life-style of a servant for his disciples to adopt. When the Twelve, hungry for splendor, argued over who among them would be the greatest, Jesus called them together and said,

> You know that the rulers of the Gentiles lord it over them, and their high officials exercise authority over them. Not so with you. Instead, whoever wants to become great among you must be your servant, and whoever wants to be first must be your slave—just as the Son of Man did not come to be served, but to serve, and to give his life a ransom for many.
>
> *Matthew 20:25-28*

Jesus saw Himself and His mission in the perspective of servanthood. Indeed, He *is* the Servant of the Lord spoken of by the prophet Isaiah and by New

100

Testament writers. Paul wrote in Philippians that Jesus,

> . . . being in very nature God,
> did not consider equality with God something to be grasped,
> but made himself nothing, taking the very nature of a servant,
> being made in human likeness.
> And being found in appearance as a man, he humbled himself
> and became obedient to death—even death on a cross!
>
> *Philippians 2:6-8*

These passages, with Isaiah's portrait, give us several distinctive impressions of the Servant.

- His desire to serve God.
- His stance before men is one of humility.
- His mission is to bring deliverance to others.
- His pathway of servanthood is followed at great personal cost.
- His strength comes from God, who upholds Him in and through His mission.

How greatly these qualities contrast with the lifestyle of Israel against which Isaiah cries. Israel's desire was selfish. Her attitude was arrogant and proud; her goal was to gather wealth and comforts for herself. The pathway she chose was whatever seemed to promise the easiest life. She failed to rely on God but relied instead on her own strength or on alliances with pagan nations around her. But only

101

the servant relies on and knows God.

The servant. There has been much debate over just who is the servant Isaiah speaks of. In some cases the prophet seems to refer to Israel. In other cases the reference is clearly to the Messiah. Some have insisted that *every* servant passage is essentially Messianic and thus speaks of Christ.

Looking through the whole Scripture, it is clear that the idea of the "servant of the Lord" is *not* reserved for the coming Messiah alone. Various prophets speak of themselves as the Lord's servants (1 Kings 18:36; 2 Sam. 7:19f). David and even Nebuchadnezzar (Jer. 17:6) are identified as servants of the Lord. The nation Israel is also specifically identified as God's servant (Isa. 49:3). But when Israel fails to fulfill her servant role, Isaiah turns to reveal a Messianic Servant who will come and accomplish salvation (49:6).

The New Testament uses the term "servant" to refer to the people of God in general (Acts 4:29; Rev. 2:20). It also refers to the community of Israel (Luke 1:54). But most often the title refers to Jesus (Matt. 12:18; Acts 3:13; 4:27, 30, etc.).

In the New Testament each believer-servant ministers to the whole community of faith, taking as his example the Lord's own servant-life (compare Mark 10:43f; 1 Cor. 4:5 with Mark 10:35-45; Matt. 23:8-12; John 13:1-17).

THE Servant. Just as it's clear that Isaiah uses "servant" to designate more than one group of individuals, it's also clear that among the servants of the Lord there is one who has a predominant place. This

Servant, unlike others, never fails to do the will of the Lord. This Servant draws on God's strength and accomplishes His purpose. This Servant is clearly the promised Messiah, the one through whom all of God's purposes for Creation will be fulfilled. Isaiah 52:13—53:12 is a clear Old Testament prophecy of Christ's death and its meaning, referred to explicitly in the New Testament ten times (Matt. 8:17; Luke 22:37; John 12:38; Acts 8:32-33; Rom. 10:16; Heb. 9:28; 1 Pet. 2:22, 24-25).

What is particularly striking in Isaiah is the fact that the God revealed in all His glorious might and splendor is also the God of the Incarnation. He comes to be Servant as well as King. In the language of paradox, the Ruler serves, and the Servant rules.

This paradox is captured in Philippians 2. The passage describes Jesus' willing descent from glory to take on the form of the Servant, and as a servant to be obedient, even to death. But His death leads to the restoration of splendor. Because He served,

> Therefore God exalted him to the highest place
>   and gave him the name that is above every
>   name,
> that at the name of Jesus every knee should bow,
>   in heaven and on earth and under the earth,
> and every tongue confess that Jesus Christ is
>   Lord,
>   to the glory of God the Father.
>
> *Philippians 2:9-11*

The Lord is the Servant. The Servant is Lord.

103

Lessons from servanthood. Jesus taught that we who believe in Him need to follow in His steps and serve one another as He served (see 1 Peter 2:21; John 13:3-17; Matt. 20:26-28). Christ called us to be servants who are faithful in our appointed tasks (see Matt. 24:45—25:30). Paul exhorts us to develop the servant's attitude (Phil. 2:1-4).

The same lessons are found in the Old Testament. God called Israel to be His servant, the agent through whom He could make Himself known to mankind. Israel arrogantly turned away from the path of obedience to the heavenly Lord. Rather than reveal God to the nations, Israel became like the nations, and her value to God and man was lost.

But God did not desert His servant Israel; instead He acted to redeem. He Himself entered the world as Immanuel, the Servant. In salvation's ultimate act of obedience, He died for Israel and called all nations to the Lord. In the Servant we find our deepest revelation of the character of God, and we meet the agent who accomplishes God's good purposes for mankind.

What does all this mean for us? We too are called to be servants, walking in Jesus' steps. As we commit ourselves to the Heavenly Lord, He will strengthen and direct us, and through us do good to all men. God's servants find fulfillment and meaning in life. But beware! The servant ministry requires a servant's heart. We must rely fully on God and prize Jesus' attitude of humility if we are looking forward to the prospect of exaltation by Him who rewards all who chose to obey.

SERVANT PORTRAITS IN ISAIAH

Isaiah contains a number of brief references to a servant (41: 8-9; 42: 19; 43: 10; 44: 1-2, 21, 26; 45: 4; 48: 20). In addition there are four main passages (42: 1-9; 49: 1-6; 50: 4-10; 52: 13—53: 12). It's helpful in understanding these middle chapters of Isaiah to look at them through the Servant's eyes. What are the characteristics of a servant?

Israel, the servant chosen by God (41: 8-9), failed to realize that the recipient of God's grace becomes an agent of God's grace. Missing this meaning of the Covenant with haughty disdain, Israel stubbornly chose a life-style of selfishness and wickedness. Now Isaiah introduces a Servant who is totally unlike Israel, a Servant who will pick up the shambles of the unfinished task and redeem not only Israel but all mankind.

Isaiah 42:1-9
"Here is my servant." These words commence a unique unveiling. Rather than a bold conqueror, the one who will accomplish God's purpose and establish justice is a Servant who

> . . . will not shout or cry out,
>   or raise his voice in the streets.
> A bruised reed he will not break,
>   and a smoldering wick he will not snuff out.
> *Isaiah 42:2-3*

The first part of this portrait is clear: the Servant will

105

not be strident or attract attention to Himself as He goes about His mission. Humility, not forcefulness, will identify Him.

But what of the second? What of the bruised reed and the smoldering wick?

The Hebrew language does not describe with abstract concepts but with vivid word pictures. The images of the bruised reed and smoldering wick would have been clear to Isaiah's readers. The bruised reed conjured up the picture of the shepherd, who selected a reed from which to make a shepherd's pipe (flute). The shepherd cut the reed, then gently tapped the bark with a smooth stone. Rotating the reed, he continued tapping. He had to be gentle, because if he bruised the reed with the stone, it would be worthless as an instrument. He would have to toss it away and begin all over again.

The same was true of smoking flax. In Isaiah's day the lamp was a small bowl of oil in which a bit of flax was dropped as a wick. After a time, the flax became encrusted with carbon. The wick began to sputter and to smoke. The wick was useless, to be plucked from the bowl and tossed out.

But to the Servant, the worthless of the world have great value! He will not casually snap or discard them; instead, He commits Himself to bring forth justice for them, until the Law of the Lord brings all men hope.

Isaiah moves on. The Creator of the heavens and earth has committed Himself to walk beside the Servant and will make the Servant Himself to be a Covenant

to open eyes that are blind,
to free captives from prison
and to release from the dungeon those who sit
in darkness.

Isaiah 42:7

Isaiah 49:1–50:3
The first seven verses of this chapter reintroduce the servant theme. Israel herself has been called by God to be "my servant—Israel, in whom I will display my splendor" (49:3). But Israel is forced to confess that she has failed and fallen far short of that purpose (49:4). Then comes a new revelation: One who was formed in the womb to be God's Servant will gather Israel again to the Lord (v. 5) and, beyond that, will become

. . . a light for the Gentiles,
that you may bring my salvation to the ends of
the earth.

Isaiah 49:6

In spite of the Servant's initial rejection by the world, God has not rejected Him. He will act through Christ in total faithfulness to His expressed purpose of doing good to all men (v. 7).

Restoration: 49:8-26. The Servant has been introduced. Now Isaiah describes the healing and restoration God will accomplish through Him. The captives will return; they will shout for joy; the Gentiles will honor the chosen people. In the punishment of oppressors

107

> . . . all mankind will know
> that I, the Lord, am your Savior,
> your Redeemer, the Mighty One of Jacob.
> *Isaiah 49:26*

While she was in captivity, Israel despaired God's favor. But had God ever divorced Himself from Israel (50:1)? Is God too weak to rescue (50:2)? No, through the Servant restoration comes, and lost hope turns to joy.

Isaiah 50:1–52:12
This passage begins with a further unveiling of the Servant (50:4-10). He is committed to *obedience.* While Israel stubbornly refuses to respond to the Lord, the Servant will be completely responsive to God's will.

Isa. 50:4. Because the Servant listens intently and obediently "morning by morning," He has wisdom to "know the word that sustains the weary." Obedience qualifies and marks the Servant as he pursues His ministry.

Isa. 50:5. The open ear (to hear) comes with obedience. The Servant can hear God's voice because "I have not been rebellious; I have not drawn back."

Isa. 50:6. The choice to obey God has brought the Servant into conflict with men. But even the most degrading of insults fails to shame or deter him: "I set my face like flint." Total commitment rests on total confidence in God: "I will not be put to shame."

Isa. 50:8-9. Rather than react vengefully, the Servant waits for God's vindication. Because the Sovereign Lord helps the Servant, no case against Him can stand. Every human opponent will "wear out like a garment," while God remains forever. *Isa. 50:10.* The Servant's obedience provides the example for Israel. All who fear the Lord will obey the word of the Servant and trust in the name of the Lord. Those who rely on God, as the Servant relies, will have deliverance.

Salvation is everlasting (Isa. 51:1-16). How comforting the Servant message is to those "who pursue righeousness, and who seek the Lord." As God's people listen, justice, righteousness, and peace will light the world. How good to know that "the cowering prisoners will soon be set free!" (v. 14).

Wrath is past (Isa. 51:17-21). In the first half of Isaiah the prophet saw the grim prospect of God's coming day of retribution. But he calls those who have experienced wrath to awake (v. 17)! God takes from their hand the cup of judgment that made them drunken. Now He calls out to them through the Servant,

> Awake, awake, O Zion,
>   clothe yourself with strength.
> Put on your garments of splendor,
>   O Jerusalem, the holy city. . . .
> Shake off your dust;
>   rise up, sit enthroned, O Jerusalem.
>
> *Isaiah 52:1-2*

The Good News is that God reigns. His return to

109

Zion will cause the people to break into songs of joy.

The way of obedience to God is not a way of bondage but of *freedom*. The ministry of the servant breaks the chains from the necks of God's people.

Leviticus 25:42 instructs that no Israelite shall be sold by another to be a slave. "For they are my servants," God says, "whom I brought forth out of the land of Egypt; they shall not be sold as slaves." The person who willingly chooses to obey God and live as His servant finds freedom from slavery.

Today, many are enslaved to anxiety, to passion, to greed, to fear of others, and to self-doubt. They can find the strength to break such chains by choosing to become God's willing servants.

Isaiah 52:13–53:12

In this final servant passage we find the Old Testament's fullest expression of Christ's mission. We also gain our deepest insight into the Servant's commitment and life-style. Because of its significance in understanding Christ's dual role as suffering Savior and glorious King, we'll examine this passage in depth in the next chapter.

What is important for us to grasp from the section we have studied is that God chose to become The Servant. In the humble things of this world the glory of our God is both hidden and disclosed.

GOING DEEPER

to personalize

1. In what ways do you think most people would

see contrasts (or conflict) between Isaiah's earlier emphases on God and his present portrait of Him as Servant?

2. Read carefully the following Isaiah "servant" passages, and then answer the question below.

Isa. 4: 8-9   Isa. 45: 4
Isa. 43: 10   Isa. 48: 20
Isa. 44: 1-2, 21, 26   Isa. 49: 1-6
                                              Isa. 50: 4-19

(a) Who is the servant referred to in each passage?
(b) What do we learn about servanthood?
(c) What do we learn about *The* Servant?

3. Jesus refers to His servant ministry in Matthew 20: 25-28, where He holds up His own servanthood as the model for His disciples.

(a) How many contrasts can you think of between the life-style of the "Gentile rulers" and the servant approach to leadership?
(b) How many comparisons can you find between these two types of leadership?
(c) In what specific ways can *you* be a servant in the fellowship of the church?

4. From your studies of the servant in Isaiah, develop five principles for daily living that fit our modern day.

to probe
Look up the word "servant" in the New Testament. What major passages deal with servanthood? Write a paper on the Christian's life as a servant.

111

THE SERVANT'S SUFFERING

ALTHOUGH IT WAS THE LORD'S WILL to crush him
and cause him to suffer,
and though the Lord makes his life a guilt offering,
he will see his offspring and prolong his days,
and the will of the Lord will prosper in his hand.
After the suffering of his soul,
he will see the light of life and be satisfied;
by his knowledge my righteous servant will justify
many.
and he will bear their iniquities.
Therefore I will give him a portion among the
great,
and he will divide the spoils with the strong,
because he poured out his life unto death,
and was numbered with the transgressors.
For he bore the sin of many,
and made intercession for the transgressors.

Isaiah 53:10-12

ALL THINGS

In Ephesians Paul views Jesus Christ as the one ordained "to bring all things in heaven and on earth together." This will be "put into effect when the times will have reached their fulfillment" (Eph. 1:10). God's design is far more complex than the saints of old, with their dreams of the righteous Kingdom, imagined. Yet all the strands of God's plan are drawn together in the person of the Messiah.

Isaiah has already touched on many aspects of God's purpose. At the time of fulfillment
- The Sovereign Lord will come with power (40:10).
- The Holy One of Israel will bring judgment upon earth (41:14-15).
- The God of Israel will make the barren land rich (41:17-18).
- The warrior Lord will triumph over all His enemies (42:13).
- The Savior will bring all Israel back from captivity to the Promised Land (43:5-6).
- Israel's King will blot out their transgressions (43:15, 25).
- The Redeemer will pour out God's Spirit on Israel's descendants (44:3, 6).
- The Servant will not only restore Israel, but Gentiles as well will know God's salvation (49:6).
- The Lord will comfort Israel and bring her joy (49:13).
- The Sovereign Lord will cause the Gentiles to

113

acknowledge the favored position of Israel as God's chosen (49: 22).

- The Righteous Lord will reestablish justice, and a holy people will light the way for all nations (51: 4-5).

These exciting visions of God's final purpose for the Jews understandably captured their imagination. Through many dreadful centuries these promises brought hope. Longing for Messiah, the restorer of Israel's glory, became the dominant theme of a Judaism that, for centuries before Christ and millennia after Him, has suffered under Gentile domination and persecution.

With these pictures of splendor in their Scripture, who would drink deeply of the pictures of judgment and suffering? With the bright prospect of a warrior King coming in power to vindicate a waiting Israel, who would dwell on the Servant? And who would pause to wonder if power *by itself* could cleanse and make pure the hearts of men whose lives were warped by the pursuit of wickedness?

But Isaiah sketches other pictures of the time of the end that must be reconciled with the visions of power and glory:

- It is a Servant who will establish justice (42: 1).
- The Servant will not "shout or cry out" or reject the worthless (42: 2-3).
- The Servant will Himself *be* the Covenant through which the people and the Gentiles find release (42: 6).
- The Servant will be despised and abhorred by the nation Israel (49: 7).

114

- The Servant as a Covenant will restore the land and free those held captive in darkness (49: 8-9).
- The Servant will live a life marked by obedience to the Lord (50: 4-5).
- The Servant will be ridiculed and attacked by those He serves (50: 6).
- Obedience to the Servant's Word and reliance on His God is the way of restoration for all men (50: 10)

But not only must we accept a Servant-King through whom God intends to bring in glory. We are suddenly jolted by the explicit picture in Isaiah 52 and 53 of the Servant's suffering.

Contrasts. The contrasts between the picture of the Sovereign Lord acting in power and the Servant puzzled Old Testament saints. Even though they realized that the Servant of Isaiah is the Messiah, they never really understood how it all fit together. As we look at the contrasts, we can understand their uncertainty.

The Sovereign Lord	The Servant
• will enforce obedience	• will be obedient
• will blot out injustice	• will suffer injustice
• will come in power	• will not raise his voice
• will judge the earth	• will not discard smoking flax
• will fulfill the Covenant promises	• will become a Covenant
• will be welcomed by Israel	• will be rejected by Israel
• will win the allegiance of all mankind	• will be mocked and spit upon

We could go on, but this is enough to help us understand the dilemma and raise the question, "How can these diverse strands of teaching be reconciled?"

From the perspective of the New Testament it's easy to see that it was always God's intention to draw all elements of His plan together in one central person, Christ (Eph. 1:10-11). The Immanuel of Isaiah, *God With Us,* entered the world to live as a Servant. In His incarnation He lived a life of obedience. He suffered, and in His suffering became Himself the New Covenant through which God will restore men to right relationship with Himself. Then, the work of redemption accomplished, this same Jesus would take up the power He had willingly laid aside. Today He sits in glory as the Sovereign Lord (Phil. 2:6-11)! In that role He will become the Judge, who is qualified not only by power but by His own demonstrated righteousness to pass sentence on sin and to bring in the time of peace for all.

The time element, which we can grasp today, was not known then. Isaiah makes no note of the millennia that would pass between the time of humbleness (42:2-3a) and the time of righteousness brought in (42:3b-4). Today, from our backward look at the cross, we realize that there are two comings of Christ. Looking ahead to the first coming, Isaiah and the others were never clear about the gap of centuries. All they knew was "He is coming." Somehow the Glorious King would also be the Suffering Servant. God intended, through the suffering of His righteous servant, to lay a new foundation for man's relationship with His God. And then the sufferer would be King.

BECOMING A COVENANT
Isaiah 52:13–53:12

Twice in Isaiah's portrait of the Servant we're told that he is to "be a covenant" (42: 6; 49: 8). Anyone familiar with the Old Testament world, as Isaiah's first readers undoubtedly were, could not miss the implications.

Covenants. Covenants were the contracts of the Old Testament world. They defined the relationship between the parties to the covenant.

The Old Testament knows two kinds of covenants made between God and men. There is the unconditional covenant, which is equivalent to a promise or oath. And there is the conditional covenant, which is equivalent to an "if, then" contract. In the conditional covenant, the failure of one party to live up to the contract's requirements frees the other part from his obligations under it.

There are three basic *unconditional* covenants in the Old Testament. The first is the Abrahamic: that great promise of God to Abraham that he and his descendants would be God's chosen. Through them the good purposes of God would be worked out.

The second is the Davidic: that promise to David that one of his descendants would be the ultimate King of prophecy.

The third is a covenant defined by Jeremiah over

117

a hundred years after the time of Isaiah. It is called the New Covenant, and focuses on the replacement of the Bible's one conditional covenant, the Mosaic. God's Law had been revealed to humanity as an objective, external standard; through a New Covenant, God's Law would one day be written on human hearts. Each of these covenants is an oath/commitment that *God promises* He *will* do.

The one conditional covenant that has a central place in the Old Testament is the Mosaic Covenant. This covenant of Law is defined as the relationship between God and men *while* mankind waited through time for the other covenants to find fulfillment at history's end. Those who responded to God as He spoke through the Law, and were obedient, found God's blessing in their present life. In the same way, disobedience would bring judgment upon them.

But when the Servant becomes a covenant, then a new pattern of relationship between God and man will be set.

Making a covenant. Looking into the Old Testament culture we see several ways of making a covenant. The most binding of all was called a "covenant of blood." The makers of this covenant sacrificed an animal and then each walked between the pieces of the sacrifice to make a totally binding commitment. The Abrahamic Covenant rested on this kind of commitment, but only God passed between the pieces of the sacrificial animals. He thus bound himself unconditionally in an act Abraham understood fully (Gen. 15).

118

In Isaiah 52 and 53 we see the making of a New Covenant: a covenant in which God's Servant is Himself the sacrifice! In becoming a covenant, and a covenant of blood at that, the Servant makes the ultimate commitment to those for whom He sacrifices Himself. The Servant is Himself the oath of God. The purposes for which He dies *will* be accomplished.

THE KEY PASSAGE

Seen in the context of covenant, the words of Isaiah 52 and 53 become strikingly clear. The identity of the Servant as Jesus is unmistakable from our perspective of history.

Isaiah 52:13-15
See, my servant will act wisely;
   he will be raised and lifted up and highly
      exalted.
Just as there were many who were appalled at
      him—
   his appearance was so disfigured beyond that of
      any man
   and his form marred beyond human likeness—
so will he sprinkle many nations,
   and kings will shut their mouths because of him.
For those who were not told will see,
   and those who have not heard will understand.

These verses introduce the final, and central, servant passage in Isaiah. He is identified as God's

Servant, and his exaltation is foretold. He is wise and yet He will make choices that seem foolish to men. He will choose a path of suffering in obedience to the Father's will. But the terrible suffering He will undergo is God's will and is for a great and vital purpose. All will stand in awe, stunned by the wisdom and the love of God, when they finally grasp the meaning of the Servant's death.

The reference to sprinkling in this passage is a reference to purifying action of the priest with the water and blood of sacrifice (see Lev. 4:6; 8:11).

Isaiah 53:1-3
> Who has believed our message
> > and to whom has the arm of the Lord been
> > > revealed?
> He grew up before him like a tender shoot,
> > and like a root out of dry ground.
> He had no beauty or majesty to attract us to him,
> > nothing in his appearance that we should desire
> > > him.
> He was despised and rejected by men,
> > a man of sorrows, and familiar with suffering.
> Like one from whom men hide their faces
> > he was despised, and we esteemed him not.

The Servant's appearance would have no attraction for those looking for the King who would dash Israel's enemies to death. Who could believe that such a person, without majesty or splendor, would be the one through whom all God's purposes would be fulfilled? To those hungry for outward glory, what

120

attraction could there be in a person
  despised
  rejected
  sorrowful
  familiar with suffering?
The prophet sees that the people in the Messiah's own time will hide their faces from Him in shame, despising Him and considering Him of no value or worth.

Isaiah 53:4-6
  Surely he took up our infirmities
    and carried our sorrows,
  yet we considered him stricken by God,
    smitten by him, and afflicted.
  But he was pierced for our transgressions,
    he was crushed for our iniquities;
  the punishment that brought us peace was upon
      him,
    and by his wounds we are healed.
  All we, like sheep, have gone astray,
    each of us has turned to his own way;
  and the Lord has laid on him
    the iniquity of us all.

Isaiah goes on to tell more of the great misunderstanding. As the Servant's path of obedience leads to deeper and deeper suffering . . . and finally to death . . . the conviction of the people grows that God has rejected Him. Yet in fact the suffering is for the sins of God's people. He took our place, bearing our weaknesses and sorrows, He was pierced for our

121

transgressions, crushed for our iniquities, punished for our rebellion, and took on his shoulders the iniquity of us all.

This suffering was not only in our place, it was for our benefit. In His great act of self-sacrifice the Servant
    brought peace
    healed
    lifted the sin-guilt from us.

As we grasp the terminology of sacrifice and the picture of the Servant as a Covenant, we see that by his death the Servant of God has brought sinners new life.

Isaiah 53:7-9
    He was oppressed and afflicted,
        yet he did not open his mouth;
    He was led like a lamb to the slaughter,
        and as a sheep before her shearers is silent,
        so he did not open his mouth.
    By oppression and judgment, he was taken away.
        And who can speak of his descendants?
    For he was cut off from the land of the living;
        for the transgression of my people he was
            stricken.
    He was assigned a grave with the wicked,
        and with the rich in his death,
    though he had done no violence,
        nor was any deceit in his mouth.

Isaiah points out that the Servant's suffering was voluntary. Under the harshest mistreatment no word of complaint came from his lips. Isaiah tells us in verses 8 and 9 what actually happened to Jesus. He was taken from arrest (*otzer*, "oppression") to an unjust trial. He died a painful death, and yet was given an honorable burial among the rich. Because he had done no violence, nor was any deceit in him, the Servant was spared the **final** disgrace intended by his enemies.

Isaiah 53:10-12

Although it was the Lord's will to crush him and
cause him to suffer,
and although the Lord makes his life a guilt
offering,
he will see his offspring and prolong his days,
and the will of the LORD will prosper in his hand.
After the suffering of his soul,
he will see the light of life and be satisfied;
by his knowledge my righteous servant will justify
many,
and he will bear their iniquities.
Therefore I will give him a portion among the
great,
and he will divide the spoils with the strong,
because he poured out his life unto death,
and was numbered with the transgressors.
For he bore the sin of many,
and made intercession for the transgressors.

While not ignoring the responsibility of the wicked men who conspired in the Servant's death, we must recognize that God Himself chose this course for His

Servant. The Servant freely elected to be a guilt offering and thus became both the Priest and Sacrifice in one.

The results for the Servant are startling. Although He dies, for the sacrifice always dies, the Servant still will
see his offspring
prolong his days
be the agent who carries out God's will for men
see the light of life
gain great satisfaction
take his place among the great
gain the treasures associated with victory.

How can a dead man continue past the time of his self-sacrifice and gain all these rewards? The resurrection of Jesus gives God's historical, definitive answer. God raised His Servant to life again; death could not hold Him captive.

But there are exciting results for men as well. They are the beneficiaries of the Servant's sacrificial act. They become His offspring, taking their place beside Him as sons of God; experience justification; and find freedom from the sins the Servant bore away.

The sweeping purposes of God for good to all mankind never neglect the individual. In fact, God's concern for the individual leads Him to the ultimate self-revelation; the exalted Sovereign Lord becomes Servant in the world He created. He wins redemption for His tormentors by becoming a sacrifice in their place. If we have wondered about the motives of this Holy Being the prophet Isaiah has described, we wonder no longer. In His humiliation we find the ultimate unveiling of love.

GOING DEEPER

to personalize
1. Read and meditate on Isaiah 52:13—53:12 for at least ten minutes before doing any other assignment.
2. Read each of the following New Testament references to Isaiah 53. Write a paragraph that summarizes the New Testament's interpretation of this passage. Matt. 8:17; Luke 22:37; John 12:38; Acts 8:32-33; Rom. 10:16; 15:21; Heb. 9:28; 1 Pet. 2:22, 24-25.
3. Hebrews 10 suggests that Christ's death was a sacrifice. Read the chapter carefully, and see what parallels exist between it and Isaiah 53.
4. 1 John 4:16-21 deals with the issue of God's motives. Compare this passage with Isaiah 52:13—53:12. What insights do you gain into God's motives? How do your own motives compare?

to probe
Use a concordance to look up passages that speak of the New Covenant. Include Jeremiah 31, Hebrews 6:13-20, and Hebrews 8. Write a paper on the meaning of the Servant as a Covenant.

THE COVENANT MAKER

SEEK THE LORD while he may be found;
   call on him while he is near.
Let the wicked forsake his way
   and the evil man his thoughts.
Let him turn to the Lord, and he will have mercy
      on him,
and to our God, and he will freely pardon.

"For my thoughts are not your thoughts,
   neither are your ways my ways,"
      declares the Lord.
As the heavens are higher than the earth,
   so are my ways higher than your ways
   and my thoughts than your thoughts.
As the rain and the snow
   come down from heaven,
and do not return to it,
   without watering the earth
and making it bud and flourish,
   so that it yields seed for sowing and bread for
      eating,

so is my word that goes out from my mouth:
    It will not return to me empty,
but shall accomplish what I desire
    and achieve the purpose for which I sent it."
Isaiah 55:6-13

Isaiah frequently returns to the thought of Covenant. God has announced His purposes as an oath. God is faithful; He will keep His covenant.

The conviction that God is faithful is a theme that finds expression often in both Testaments. The psalmist sings of God's steadfast, "forever" love and praises God for the promise that

I will not remove from him my steadfast love,
    or be false to my faithfulness.
I will not violate my covenant,
    or alter the word that went forth from my lips.
Psalm 89:33-34

The New Testament writer says that a covenant

puts an end to all argument. Because God wanted to make the unchanging nature of his purpose very clear to the heirs of what was promised, he confirmed it with an oath. God did this so that, by two unchangeable things in which it is impossible for God to lie, we who have fled to take hold of the hope offered to us may be greatly encouraged. We have this hope as an anchor for the soul, firm and secure.
Hebrews 6:16-19

127

God's Word is itself a Covenant. God, who is faithful, *will* bring every announced purpose to pass.

It's important for us to know His Word, for it's there that the faithful God has revealed His thoughts and ways to us. We must learn to adjust our way of thinking to His, and our manner of life to His. God the Creator made us: God the Covenant-Giver shows us how to live. We can confidently accept His Word as a trustworthy guide.

A timeless guide. Much of the Old Testament has specific space/time impact for a given generation of God's people. Its application to a later generation is indirect. Thus, for instance, the ceremonial laws found in the Pentateuch help us see ourselves as a holy and set-apart people—but we do not observe the ceremonies today.

Yet some passages are timeless in character: they express the purposes of God in a word that rings with present urgency, because its primary impact is *now* as well as *then.* Speaking in his own time to his own people, Isaiah often rises above his own culture and speaks across millennia and cultures to men and women of every society. Many of the chapters we're exploring in this study are of that nature. The mention of "Zion" and "Jerusalem" and "Israel" fades, and the good news of how God deals with men of all generations comes into sharp relief.

Through it all we have the settled confidence that God the Maker is also the God of Covenant. The Faithful One will keep His oath, and His living Word will remain relevant and reliable until the end of time.

TIMELESS PRINCIPLES
Isaiah 54–59

What are some of the timeless principles of God's dealings with men, and how do they affect our lives?

Permanence of relationship (Isaiah 54). Isaiah moves to the analogy of marriage. God's people are the wife; God, the Maker, is the loving husband (54:5).

Unfaithful Israel, portrayed as a straying wife, is a symbol often used by the prophets. Captivated by idolatry, God's people strayed from Him like a harlot.

> You have played the harlot, forsaking your God.
> You have loved a harlot's hire
> upon all threshing floors.
>
> *Hosea 9:1*

But God's judgments are not merely retributive, but are also restorative. In spite of the disgrace and suffering that must come, God has not deserted the one to whom He has made His commitment:

> "For a brief moment I abandoned you,
> but with deep compassion I will bring you back.
> In a surge of anger
> I hid my face from you for a moment,
> but with everlasting kindness
> I will have compassion on you"
> says the Lord your Redeemer.
>
> *Isaiah 54:7-8*

God affirms the meaning of the covenant relation-

129

ship: "My unfailing love for you will not be shaken, nor my covenant of peace be removed" (54: 10). The days of discipline are meant to heal the strained relationship. The love-commitment of God to those He affirms as His own remains unshakable.

Jesus taught His disciples that in marriage a man and woman "are no longer two, but one. Therefore what God has joined together, let man not separate" (Matt. 19: 6). In marriage two individuals unite their lives, in some mysterious way becoming one. They are linked for all time in a shared identity and common purpose. Paul says of the relationship between husband and wife, "This is a profound mystery," and he says it reflects the relationship between Christ and His Church (Eph. 5: 32).

God has united believers to Him in this same kind of union which, because of His faithfulness, will never suffer the fate of so many human marriages.

We need this assurance of God's love-commitment. It's so easy when we fail Him, or when suffering comes, to doubt our relationship. We wonder if God, in a flash of anger, has melted the bonds that hold us to Him. But God is for us; therefore we shall never be separated from the love of Christ. "I am convinced," says Paul,

that neither death nor life, neither angels nor demons, neither the present nor the future, nor any powers, neither height nor depth, nor anything else in all creation, will be able to separate us from the love of God that is in Christ Jesus our Lord.

Romans 8:38-39

Open invitation (Isaiah 55). The nation to whom Isaiah preached failed to respond to the prophet's message. The state continued on its journey toward judgment. *But an open invitation was given to individuals!* Isaiah calls to those who do recognize their need,

Come, all you who are thirsty,
    come to the waters;
and you who have no money,
    come, buy and eat!

Isaiah 55:1

The person who hears the invitation is to respond in faith and come into a covenant relationship with God. In that relationship, the benefits of the promise (which will one day be given to all) will become the present possession of the individual now.

Give ear and come to me;
    hear me, that your soul may live.
I will make an everlasting covenant with you,
    my unfailing kindnesses promised David.

Isaiah 55:3

This invitation is open to all, including the wicked man, who is invited to forsake his way and his evil thoughts. To every individual who comes, God promises to have mercy on him and to freely pardon (55:7).

It is at this point that God declares, "My thoughts are not your thoughts, neither are your ways my ways" (55:8). God does not deal with us on our

131

terms, but on His. Jesus picks up this same theme in His instruction to His disciples to love their enemies when He pointed out,

> (God) causes his sun to rise on the evil and the good, and sends rain on the righteous and the unrighteous. If you love those who love you, what reward will you get? Are not even the tax collectors doing that? And if you greet only your brothers, what are you doing more than others? Do not even pagans do that? Be perfect, therefore, as your heavenly Father is perfect.
> *Matthew 5:45-48*

God initiates relationship with those who are His enemies, and does so with love. As His people, we too are to take the initiative and to love aggressively. In order to have this kind of loving involvement with others, we must look to God for our example, because loving others is foreign to mankind.

God's invitation to the wicked promises that when they respond to Him, life-change will follow; they will have joy, peace, and fruitfulness (Isa. 55:12-13).

The excluded welcomed (Isaiah 56). In chapter 55 the individuals within the chosen nation respond to God and find the blessing to which the crowd is blind. Now the prophet makes it clear that more than just the chosen people are invited to have salvation.

> Let no foreigner who has joined himself to the
> Lord say,
> "The Lord will surely exclude me from his
> people."

132

And let not any eunuch complain,
"I am only a dry tree."

Isaiah 56:3

According to the Mosaic Law both foreigners and eunuchs were excluded from worship. There was the promise that someday, at the time of the end, all nations could taste of God's salvation. That blessing was to await the work of Messiah.

But God wants to let the excluded know that they are welcome *now*.

Their burnt offerings and sacrifices
  will be accepted on my altar;
for my house will be called
  a house of prayer for all nations.
The Sovereign Lord declares—
  he who gathers the exiles of Israel:
"I will gather still others to them
  besides those already gathered."

Isaiah 56:7-8

History shows this principle in operation. Rahab in the days of Joshua, Ruth in the later day of the Captivity: all these were pagans who responded to God and who found a place in His love. Even that wicked city, Nineveh, which repented under the prophetic ministry of Jonah, finds a place in the Bible record.

The New Testament explains that those once "excluded from citizenship in Israel and foreigners to the covenants of the promise, without hope and without God in the world" have now been "brought near through the blood of Christ" (Eph. 2:12-13). The unexpected dimension of God's promise is His intention to "create in himself one new man out of the two, thus making peace" (Eph. 2:15). Not only are the excluded welcomed, they are welcomed on the same terms and to the same inheritance as the chosen!

We have a tendency to deal with the excluded as if they were really different from us, so different that to be acceptable they must first become like us. God accepts each person as he is, whether foreigner or eunuch, and brings him and us together into the New Covenant that Christ *is*. When we evaluate others on the basis of how they are different from us, rather than seeking to affirm our potential oneness in and through Christ, we miss the wonder of our Covenant-keeping and Covenant-making God.

Restoration's way (Isa. 57). Why do righteous people sometimes pass from the scene when they are most needed in society? Isaiah's insight into this problem is:

> The righteous are taken away
>   to be spared from evil.
> Those who walk uprightly
>   enter into peace;
>   they find rest as they lie in death.
>
> *Isaiah 57:1-2*

In contrast, the majority of Israelites could not be considered righteous. In fact, God declares Israel to

134

be the offspring of adulterers, prostitutes and sor-
ceresses! (v. 3). She had turned from God, who had
entered into a marriage covenant with her, and had
actively, even lustfully, sought out foreign gods (vv.
4-9). Since God did not act in judgment immediately, Israel assumed she was safe. But God warned that
He would expose her "righteousness and works"
and that neither would save His wayward people (v.
12).

God says, however, that restoration is possible.
"The man who makes me his refuge," He explains,
"will inherit the land and possess my holy mountain"
(v. 13). God will restore and build up His people
when their life-style and attitude is acceptable:

> I live . . . with him who is contrite and lowly in
>   spirit,
> to revive the spirit of the lowly
>   and to revive the heart of the contrite.
>
> *Isaiah 57:15*

God promises peace, healing, guidance, comfort,
and an attitude of praise to those who depend on
Him (vv. 18-19). While there is no peace for the
wicked (vv. 20-21), a right relationship with God will
bring inner (and even international) peace.

That relationship frees us to look beyond circumstances, and "by prayer and petition, with
thanksgiving present [our] requests to God. And the
peace of God, which transcends all understanding,
will guard [our] hearts and [our] minds in Christ
Jesus" (Phil. 4:6-7).

Faith's life-style (Isa. 58). Too often a Christian's life-style is one of ritual observance of "religious" behaviors. The people of Isaiah's day carefully fasted and followed the prescribed rituals, complaining that God did not seem to hear them. The answer?

> Yet on the day of your fasting, you do as you
>   please,
>   and you exploit all your workers.
> Your fasting ends in quarreling and strife,
>   and in striking each other with wicked fists.
> You cannot fast as you do today
>   and expect your voice to be heard on high.
>   *Isaiah 58:3-4*

What kind of "fasting" does God call us to? Isaiah goes on, relaying God's message.

> Is not this the kind of fasting I have chosen:
> to loose the chains of injustice
>   and untie the cords of the yoke,
> to set the oppressed free
>   and break every yoke?
> Is it not to share your food with the hungry
>   and to provide the poor wanderer with shelter?
>   *Isaiah 58:5-7*

The one who finds restoration and peace in Covenant relationship with God will express that commitment by sharing God's love with people. His worship may contain ritual elements, fastings, and festivals. These are not wrong. But the heart of his life-style will continue to be lovingly representing God to the world.

Repentance and redemption (Isa. 59). How bad is bad, and what is God going to do about it? Isaiah summarizes the iniquities which have separated Israel from God. The only way to get the full impact of the strength and beauty of his words is to read the passage for yourself. So right now read aloud (preferably in a modern translation) verses 1-15.

Notice how far Israel was from God's intention for her:

> The way of peace they do not know;
>   there is no justice in their paths.
> They have turned them into crooked roads;
>   no one who walks in them will know peace.
>
> *Isaiah 59:8*

God Himself must intercede and redeem. His own arm works salvation. When the Redeemer comes to Zion and the Covenant is established, then not only will sins stand forgiven, but the words of God and His Spirit will become one with God's people.

Where there is sin, oppression, injustice, or thoughtless arrogance that dismisses and discards other human beings, then God must act. For those who remain hardened there will be retribution (57:18), but God's deepest desire is to redeem. And so we are called to enter into a covenant of peace and personal relationship with God. He then will change the hardness of our hearts and plant within us His living Word.

GOING DEEPER

to personalize

Each of the following chapters is a statement of principles concerning God's thoughts and ways. Select one of them, and see what parallel principles you can find in both Old and New Testaments:

- Isaiah 54: "marital" relationship between God and His people
- Isaiah 55: open invitation to individuals to appropriate salvation
- Isaiah 56: the excluded welcomed by God
- Isaiah 58: faith's life-style as more than outward religious observance
- Isaiah 59: the nature of sin

For the chapter you choose:

1. Outline the key elements of its message.

2. Give at least five parallel passages from Old or New Testaments.

3. Summarize its message as God's voice to *you* today.

THE LORD OF GLORY

ARISE, SHINE! For your light has come,
  and the glory of the Lord rises upon you.
See, darkness covers the earth
  and thick darkness is over the peoples,
but the Lord rises upon you
  and his glory appears over you.
Nations will come to your light,
  and kings to the brightness of your dawn.

Isaiah 60:1-3

Isaiah's prophecy lifts high the torch, who is the Lord Himself. In Him, Israel and all peoples find hope for the dawning of a new day.

Isaiah 1—35 focused on the deep needs that existed in the prophet's day. Against a backdrop of human arrogance, oppression, sin, injustice, and fear of surrounding nations, Isaiah portrayed God as Holy One, Sovereign Lord, Judge, and Savior. In spite of flashes of hope, the overall tone of these visions of God is one of gloom and dark anger, striking terror into the heart of arrogant Judah.

But now in chapters 40—66 the focus is not on God as He is about to act in Judah's immediate future. Isaiah looks through time to see how God will act for man at history's end, and he speaks of purpose and of hope.

In Isaiah 40—48 we saw the Everlasting God announce beforehand what He intends to bring to pass. Then He Himself moves out into that future to guarantee that His promises will be fulfilled. The great message of the Everlasting God to Israel is one of comfort, "for her hard service has been completed" (40: 1).

Then in Isaiah 49—53 we met God as Servant. Israel failed in her servant task of bringing light to the Gentiles, so God Himself accepts the Servant role. As Messiah-Servant, He steps into history to overcome sin and to "bring my salvation to the ends of the earth" (49: 6).

Isaiah 52: 12—53: 12 shows us the extent of God's Servant role. He both offers and is the sacrifice. By His death the promised Servant-Messiah wins freedom for the captive and brings many into the family of God. Passing through death, the Servant comes again to life. He will enjoy eternal fellowship with His redeemed ones.

In Isaiah 54—59 God presented Himself as Covenant Maker. He announces timeless principles of His relationship with people. Because His commitment to us and love for us is unchanging, we can be sure that redemption's promise will be kept.

And now, in the last chapters of Isaiah, we catch a glimpse of the day toward which history is moving. God's intention for us is glory. At the end of time we will discover at last the full meaning of God's good plan for His own. There we will see and share His glory. There all of life's mysteries will find final resolution in joy.

PORTRAIT OF HISTORY'S END
Isaiah 60–66

The sleepers awake (Isa. 60). The feeling we get reading Isaiah 60 is that God's people have been dozing and dreaming as they drifted along the stream of time. Then, cutting through their dreams comes a vibrant call:

> Arise, shine! For your light has come,
> and the glory of the Lord rises upon you.
> *Isaiah 60:1*

Israel's newly opened eyes see a stunning sight. From all around the sons and daughters that were lost are gathering. The riches of the nations are brought to Israel. They see God's glorious temple not on time's horizon, but here!

> You will look and be radiant,
> your heart will throb and swell with joy.
> *Isaiah 60:5*

The once-forsaken and hated shake off depression

141

as they become the pride of mankind. Most wonderful of all, in those days of spendor, God promises,

> The sun will no more be your light by day,
>   nor will the brightness of the moon shine on
>   you,
> for the Lord will be your everlasting light,
>   and your God will be your glory.
> Your sun will never set again,
>   and your moon will wane no more;
> the Lord will be your everlasting light,
>   and your days of sorrow will end.
>
> *Isaiah 60:19-20*

Ruins restored (Isaiah 61–62). The good news of
time's end focuses on restoration. The man of God is
anointed

> . . . to bind up the broken-hearted,
>   to proclaim freedom for the captives
>   and recovery of sight for the prisoners.
>
> *Isaiah 61:1*

All who mourn are comforted with the word that the
ancient ruins will be restored and the devastated
lands will be made fruitful.

Isaiah makes it clear that this picture of restoration is not primarily physical but spiritual: Its first
concern is to clothe men "with garments of salvation,
and array . . . in a robe of righteousness" (61:10).
When the Lord makes "righteousness and praise
spring up before all nations" (61:11), then the days

142

of endless blessing will come. When the Savior steps into full view,

> They will be called The Holy People,
> The Redeemed of the Lord;
> and you will be called Sought After,
> The City No Longer Deserted.
>
> *Isaiah 62:12*

The land and the people will be filled with praise.

Yearnings satisfied (Isa. 63–64). These chapters begin with God's great saving acts at the end of time. His purifying judgments precede the days of blessing (63:1-6). "I looked, but there was no helper, I was appalled that no one gave support; so my own arm worked salvation for me, and my own wrath sustained me" (63:5).

When God has completed His final act of judgment, His restored people praise Him (63:7-10).

> I will tell of the kindnesses of the Lord,
> the deeds for which He is to be praised,
> according to all the Lord has done for us.
>
> *Isaiah 63:7*

Then comes a recapitulation of their feelings before they had experienced God's salvation (63:11—64:12). They remember the days of longing. They remember the times of sin, of repentance, of desire for God once again to "rend the heavens and come down" (64:1). In the prophet's eyes, God

143

has already acted. All those longings have now been answered. The emptiness is only a dim memory. For the glory of the Lord *has* come down, and His splendor shines all around.

   God's response reviewed (Isa. 65). Now God responds to the cry of His people. Throughout history God has revealed Himself, although His people stubbornly rejected the message. To those who rejected, judgment came.

> But as for you who forsake the Lord
>   and forget my holy mountain,
> who spread a table for fortune
>   and fill bowls of mixed wine for Destiny,
> I will destine you for the sword,
>   and you will all bend down for the slaughter;
> for I called but you did not answer,
>   I spoke but you did not listen.
>
> *Isaiah 65:11-12*

To those who did respond to God's message, He gives bountifully:

> Behold, I will create
>   new heavens and a new earth.
> The former things will not be remembered,
>   nor will they come to mind.
> But be glad and rejoice forever
>   in what I will create,
> for I will create Jerusalem to be a delight
>   and its people a joy.
>
> *Isaiah 65:17-18*

The glory of God, and His presence, makes all things new.

Judgment and hope (Isa. 66). The book of Isaiah ends with a repetition of the twin themes that mark not only his message but the writings of all the prophets.

God sets before men a clear vision of two pathways. One leads to judgment, the other to hope. Each man chooses the path he will follow. Of those who turn from Him the Lord says,

> They have chosen their own ways,
>   and their souls delight in their abominations;
> so I also will choose harsh treatment for them
>   and will bring upon them what they dread.
> *Isaiah 66:3-4*

Yet the birthpangs of judgment can bring forth joy. The Lord says a day will come when all people who have responded to Him will live in fellowship with each other and with their God:

> I will extend peace to her like a river . . .
> As a mother comforts her child,
>   so will I comfort you;
>   and you will be comforted over Jerusalem.
> *Isaiah 66:12-13*

Those two ways of judgment and hope remain today. And the end of each pathway is sure.

"As the new heavens and the new earth that I

make will endure before me," declares the Lord, "so will your name and descendants endure. From one New Moon to another and from one Sabbath to another, all mankind will come and bow down before me," says the Lord. "And they will go out and look upon the dead bodies of those who rebelled against me; their worm will not die, nor will their fire be quenched, and they will be loathsome to all mankind."

Isaiah 66:22-24

The end of each pathway is sure. The choice is still ours.

GOING DEEPER

to personalize

1. Read through these last seven chapters of Isaiah. Underline any passage that seems to you to reflect the splendor of time's end.

2. Choose one of the following passages to study closely: Isa. 60:4-7; Isa. 61:1-4. Write a commentary on it, thinking particularly of how each segment would minister to the reader of Isaiah's day—and to the reader today.

3. Memorize some of the following:

● Isa. 60:19-20   ● Isa. 66:12-13
● Isa. 65:17-18   ● Isa. 66:22-23

4. Isaiah 65:20-25 reveals God's desire for mankind that has been thwarted by human sin and rebellion. Study the passage carefully and write a paragraph describing God's goals.

146

to probe

1. The Old Testament picture of the future is incomplete. In some places it seems to draw attention to God's restoration of this world under Messiah's reign. In other passages it seems to hint at a new heaven and earth beyond time. Using a concordance and any other sources you wish, what can you find out about the Old Testament picture of eternity?

2. Some have suggested that the Old Testament reflects no resurrection teaching. Others see many references to a resurrection hope. What can you find? And how does it fit with the optimism of these last chapters of Isaiah?

OLD TESTAMENT REVIEW

THE GOOD THINGS
HE HAS DONE

I WILL TELL the kindnesses of the Lord,
   the deeds for which he is to be praised,
   according to all the Lord has done for us—
yes, the many good things he had done
   for the house of Israel,
   according to his compassion and many
   kindnesses. . . .
[He] sent his glorious arm of power
   to be at Moses' right hand,
who divided the waters before them,
   to gain for himself everlasting renown.
                  Isaiah 63:7, 12

God's revelation of Himself includes His great
pivotal acts of intervention in history.

The Old Testament covers hundreds and hundreds of years. The first books were written about

I. PRIMEVAL PERIOD	CREATION Creation to Abraham	*Genesis 1–11* *Job*
II. PATRIARCHAL PERIOD (2166-1446)*	COVENANT Abraham to Moses	*Genesis 12–50*
III. EXODUS PERIOD (1446-1406)	LAW Moses' Leadership	*Exodus* *Numbers* *Leviticus* *Deuteronomy*
IV. CONQUEST OF CANAAN (1406-1390)	CONQUEST Joshua's Leadership	*Joshua*
V. TIME OF JUDGES (1367-1050)	JUDGES No Leadership	*Judges* *Ruth* *I Samuel 1–7*
VI. UNITED KINGDOM (1050-931)	KINGDOM Monarchy Established Establishment (David) Decline (Solomon)	*I Samuel 8–11* *II Samuel 1–24* *I Kings 1–11* *I Chronicles* *II Chronicles* *Psalms* *Ecclesiastes* *Proverbs* *Song of Solomon*

*Th ... adapted in part from *A Survey of Israel's History* by Leon Wood (Grand Rapids: Zondervan, 1975)

	PROPHETIC MOVEMENT	
VII. DIVIDED KINGDOM (931–586) Israel Elijah Elisha Judah	Two Kingdoms	I Kings 12–22 II Kings 1–17 II Chronicles 10–29 Jonah Obadiah Amos Hosea Micah Joel Isaiah
VIII. SURVIVING KINGDOM (722–586)	Judah Remains	II Kings 18–25 II Chronicles 30–36 Jeremiah Nahum Zephaniah Habakkuk
IX. BABYLONIAN CAPTIVITY (586–538)	JUDGMENT Torn from Palestine	Ezekiel Daniel Esther
X. RESTORATION (538–400)	The Jews Return 400 Years Between the Testaments	Ezra Nehemiah Haggai Zechariah Malachi

153

fourteen hundred years before Christ, and the last some four hundred years before Christ. Yet the events of which it speaks have roots much deeper in history. The Old Testament gradually unfolds a progressive revelation of God's person and His plan, beginning with the Creation and continuing with the formation of the Jewish people at Abraham's call (ca. 2100 B.C.).

EARLY EARTH

Text: Genesis 1—11; Job
Events: Creation, Fall, Flood
To sample, read: Gen. 2. How did God's action show that people truly are special to Him? (See Gen. 1: 27-28; Gen. 4.) What were the results of the Fall in human personality and society? (See Gen. 2: 16-17.)

Beginnings. Where did the human race come from? Why are we different from the animals? How are we different? How can we explain people's capacity to love and to hate, to do good and evil? And what about the pull we all seem to feel toward religion—toward the development of some sort of belief in the supernatural?

The Bible answers these questions in a very different way from other early writings. While early Sumerian creation myths, for example, picture the grotesque bodies of murdered gods spawning men, the Bible speaks of a God who is distinct from the physical universe, yet is the Creator of all that exists.

154

Rather than being the accidental result of a brutal crime, man is seen in the Bible as the focus of God's personal concern and purpose.

Visit a strange planet. If we read Genesis carefully, we become aware of the fact that early Earth was strikingly different from the planet we know. The waters that now fill our seas were apparently divided between earth and atmosphere, and earth was covered by heavy clouds like Venus (Gen. 1:6). There was no rain (2:5), and some have suggested that the long lives of the pre-Flood men (see Gen. 5) may have been due to the filtering of cosmic radiation by this water-vapor canopy. Earth seems to have been very different then, and we'd like to know more about it than the Bible tells!

You are what's important. Why doesn't the Bible tell us more about early Earth? Because God keeps the focus on what is important. When we read the early Genesis chapters, we get the message: it's *people* that are important to God, people like you and me.

Genesis 1 sketches, in a quick survey, God's act of creating and shaping the physical universe. Chapter 2 then explains that act in terms of God's purpose. Earth was carefully designed to be a home for man. When all was ready, God (the Father speaking to Son and Spirit) said, "Let us make man in our image, after our likeness; and let them have dominion over the flesh of the sea . . . and over all the earth" (Gen 1:26).

How do the first pages of the Bible answer that nagging question, "Who am I?" They say you are a person, special because you have been created in

God's image. It's this divine image that sets you apart from the animal creation and gives you capacities to think and feel . . . and worship.

Only the Bible offers a meaningful answer to this most basic of questions about the nature of man. Only the Bible helps us see ourselves as something more than "evolved animals." We can feel good about ourselves when we know we are persons shaped in God's image. We are special. *You* are special. Whatever you've done, whatever your inadequacies, you still are stamped with the image of God (see Gen. 9: 6—the image is retained after the Fall; see also James 3: 9).

Step up, fall down. God set newly created man and woman (Adam and Eve) in an ideal environment, the Garden of Eden, and provided for every need, even the need for work. He gave them the freedom to make their own decisions.

Genesis 3 tells us how they used that freedom: they chose to disobey God. At that moment, sin entered our world, warping human personality and distorting all human societies. The Bible tells us they were trying to step up, to "be like God" (3: 5). They apparently forgot they *were* like God, formed in His image. As they tried to climb the status ladder, they tumbled off a precipice. And it's been a long fall down, for all of us.

What has sin done? Genesis 4 sketches its impact. Adam's son, Cain, moved by hatred and jealousy, murdered his brother Abel. The first civilization distorted God's plan for sex and marriage and justified murder. The rest of human history—the wars, crimes and cruelty, and even the petty anger and antagonism that mark our daily lives—provides a demonstration of how terrible sin and its results are.

Man exercised his freedom of choice until the whole earth was filled with corruption and violence (Gen. 6:11). Then, in a cataclysmic flood that changed the form of our world, God destroyed all but Noah's family. He had judged sin without destroying mankind. God had preserved the human race, and when the ark that carried Noah and the animals came to rest on land, men and women stepped out to begin again.

Try again? This start too ended in failure (Gen. 9:18—11:9). Noah's descendants were just as disobedient and willful as earlier man. Sin's warp remained, twisting man's personality out of the shape God intended for it. Man chose not to follow the pattern that would have brought peace and joy to us all.

THE COVENANT FLAME

Date: about 2100 B.C.

Text: Genesis 12—50

Events: Abraham's call, Covenant

To sample, read: Gen. 12:1-9; 15:1-18. What did God promise Abraham, and what makes us sure He will keep that promise? Also, Gen. 37:1—46:7 is a real adventure story. Why not read it?

The Covenant. After the great Flood, the world quickly drifted back to paganism. There were traditions and stories about God, but soon, as we see in the myths of ancient civilizations, these stories became distorted and the truth was clouded by error.

But God, in His wisdom, acted upon His plan to set every thing right. He would choose a man and work through this man's descendants to bring salvation both to individuals and to society.

One man. God spoke to a man in the city of Ur, where the people worshiped the moon as a god. He told this man, Abraham, to leave his home, relatives, and comforts (for Ur was a prosperous and civilized place in Abraham's day) and to go to a land that God would point out. And Abraham did.

As the rest of the Old Testament unfolds, we see God had great things in mind. Through Abraham and his descendants, God would show all humanity what He is like. He would give a written revelation (our Bible) of His plans and His Person. And in every step of the history of one branch of this family, the Israelites, God would verify what He said about Himself.

Through this people, God would come into the world Himself! As Jesus Christ, He would die in order to settle the sin question once and for all. What's more, this same God-man will one day rule on earth as King and bring righteousness to all people.

But Abraham could not know all this. God's plan was to unfold slowly through the centuries. All Abraham could know was that God wanted to begin a great undertaking, and He wanted Abraham to take part.

Sometimes it's like this for us. God has to start somewhere to do the great things He intends. He may want to start with you! How exciting to launch out, as Abraham did, with faith and in obedience, and discover day by day where God's great adventure leads.

It's a promise. In Genesis 12, 15, and 17 we find a promise that is central to our understanding of the Old Testament. God announced to Abraham what He intended to do for and through Abraham's descendants. He promised

● to make Abraham a great nation (Gen. 12:2)
● to bless Abraham and his name (Gen. 12:2)
● to make Abraham a blessing (Gen. 12:2)
● to bless and curse others based on how they treat Abraham's descendants (Gen. 12:3)
● to bless all mankind through Abraham (Gen. 12:3)
● to give a special land to Abraham's descendants (Gen. 12:7; 15:18-19)

Each of these promises is amplified and explained as God continued to deal with Abraham's descendants in Old Testament times. Some of the ways God would keep these promises were hidden from Abraham but are known to us. For instance, we know that the promise to bless all mankind was fulfilled as Jesus, coming in Abraham's lineage, died on the cross in order to bring us into God's family. One of the joys of studying the Old Testament is to see how, step by step, God unfolds His plan for keeping His promises to Abraham.

159

Certified and for sure. Genesis 15 helps us see how certain God's promise is. As we discussed in chapter 9, God bound Himself to fulfill His promises by the strongest contract known. He laid no conditions on Abraham for his part. It was an unconditional Covenant.

Israelites have found their identity through the centuries by looking back to this Covenant promise. They are the people of the promise, the chosen people.

As a descendant of Abraham, the Israelite also felt confidence in his relationship with God, for He was "the God of Abraham and Isaac and Jacob." We need to remember when we read the Old Testament that, while we're reading a book that is *for* us, it is *about* Israel and Israel's God. He is their God because He chose to be, and through His relationship with this people He calls all of us to come to Him.

Preview. It's a good thing that God's promise to Abraham and his progeny was unconditional. History shows God's people consistently rebelling against and rejecting Him. God, on the other hand, continues to care for His people and remains true to His promise.

When we realize just how trustworthy God is, we can relax. Knowing that God is trustworthy and having faith in Him are two sides of the same coin.

The rest of Genesis tells of Abraham's son Isaac and grandson Jacob. These men inherited God's promise and passed it on to their children, who would become the nation of Israel and inherit the Promised Land.

THE SEA OPENS

Date: about 1450 B.C.
Text: Exodus, Leviticus, Numbers, Deuteronomy
Events: deliverance; the giving of the Law and sacrificial system
To sample, read: Exod. 6: 2-13; 8—12. See how God acts to keep His covenant promise. Also Lev. 19. What did holy living involve in Old Testament days? Is it very different now?

The historical trail of the patriarchs (Abraham, Isaac, and Jacob) leads to Egypt. The family went down from the Promised Land to Egypt during a time of famine—and stayed there for 400 years. At first they were guests, but as their numbers grew and the years passed, they became slaves.

Why slavery? It must not have seemed worthwhile to be the chosen people, but God did have a purpose in this long interlude. The Israelites who made up the original colony numbered 74; in some 400 years they grew to nearly 2 million, with 600,000 men (Exod. 12: 37). This growth could not have occurred had they remained in Palestine, which was a battlefield for the great empires (Egypt, the Hittites). It was already inhabited by peoples who would have resisted the growth of a new nation and who might well have attempted to destroy them while they were still small. In Egypt the people suffered, especially toward the end, but by then they had already multiplied and had become a great nation.

God gets involved. When the time was right, God chose a man, Moses, to lead His people out of slav-

161

ery. Exodus records how God became directly involved in His people's deliverance, showing His power to the Israelites and to the Egyptians. When Pharaoh refused to let the Israelite slaves go, God brought a series of plagues on the land. At Moses' command gnats and flies, lice, frogs, killing hail, the bloody Nile, darkness, boils, and locusts gave testimony to God's power and His concern for His people. Finally, God brought death into the homes of the Egyptians, striking down the firstborn in each family, before the Pharaoh would release Israel.

God led His people in a personal and visible way out of Egypt, pausing to destroy the Egyptian army that Pharaoh sent after them. The sea that miraculously opened for Israel closed on the pursuing hordes, and the enemy was destroyed.

Through these events, the Hebrews (Exod. 6:1-7) and the Egyptians (Exod. 7:5) learned who God really is, and the false gods of Egypt were judged worthless (Exod. 12:12).

Critical elements. This fifty-year period included

• The Exodus: God remembered and delivered His people.

• The Passover: Before the death angel passed across the land in the final plague to kill the Egyptian firstborn, the Hebrews sprinkled on the doorposts of their homes the blood of a sacrificial lamb. Seeing the blood, the death angel passed over Hebrew homes.

Even today this event is remembered annually by Jews, most of whom are not aware that the blood speaks graphically of Christ's sacrifice for us.

162

● The Law: God led the Hebrew people to Mt. Sinai, where He gave the Law (see the next section). The Law shows what is right, but makes the law-breaker guilty.

● The sacrificial system: Immediately after giving the Law, God instituted a place of worship and sacrifice (Exod. 24—40). The blood sacrifice made an atonement (covering) for sin (Lev. 17:11). With his sin covered, a sinner could approach God and be sure of acceptance. God's way is always a way of forgiveness, not perfection. You and I fall short too. How good to know that God will accept us because of our sacrifice, Jesus Christ.

● New Life: The regulations in parts of Exodus and Leviticus showed the people how to live holy and pure lives. God also gave them guidelines for social life, for religious expression, for family life, and for political and economic life. His goal was to give them concrete examples of how they might live to express love to God, to one another, and even to pagan peoples who might come among them.

The laws may seem strange at some points to us. But they were far beyond other laws of the time, and some were truly touching, such as the law that no one who left his coat as collateral for a debt could be required to leave it overnight. He might need it for a blanket. It truly was a new way of life, a way of love and justice, that God had in mind for His people.

In focus. The Israelites began to get a clearer picture of God's character as they saw Him at work in their midst. They saw that He cares for people enough to get personally involved. Through the

163

Law they found out what holiness is and that God cares how people live. But still, with the demands of holiness, came the mercy of forgiveness. As we study the way of life God decreed for His people, we realize two things: He cares about *justice,* and He cares about *us.* How much happier each of us would be if we lived as lovingly and fairly as God commanded.

MOUNT SINAI

Date: about 1450-1050 B.C.
Text: Exodus, Deuteronomy, Joshua, Judges, Ruth
Events: Law Covenant given, wanderings, conquest, defeat
To sample, read: Exod. 19—20 (the Ten Commandments). Deut. 28 (No one can say that God didn't warn them!). Josh. 6—9 (evidence that obedience brings victory, disobedience defeat). Judg. 17—21 (What happens when a people ignore God's laws? Look here first, then read today's newspaper!).

Stop! My aunt got a ticket at an intersection she drove through daily. Overnight they had put up a stop sign. What she had done the day before had not been illegal. But now it was.

That's just about how the Law came into the picture. On the way out of Egypt, the Hebrew people kept murmuring, complaining, and rebelling, no matter what God did (Exod. 13—17). Though they were sinning, they couldn't really be charged with breaking any law (see Rom. 2:12-16; 7:7-13). But they weren't getting any better; in fact, both their attitude and their behavior got worse. God introduced the Law to let them know what He expected from them and what would be good for them.

This time, it's "if." Unlike the Abrahamic Covenant, the Covenant of Law was conditional. If the people obeyed, God would bless. If not, He would punish. This was a covenant between *both* parties that the people entered voluntarily. It was to be a temporary covenant, in effect only until Christ came (Gal. 3:23-26; Heb. 8:6-13). What, then, was its purpose?

God made a promise to Abraham that included elements not to be fulfilled during his lifetime. As he looked at this promise for the future, a believing Jew in Old Testament days might well have asked, "What about me now? I may be dead when that promise is finally kept. Don't I get any benefits?"

It's as if your father set up a trust fund of a million dollars to be given to you at age twenty-one. Having a million *then* doesn't give you cash *now.* To solve this problem, trust funds often authorize the beneficiary receive the interest yearly. You don't have the total sum yet, but you do get its benefits.

It was like this for the Israelites. God's promise to Abraham was money in the bank, something they could count on. And, *if a given generation kept the Law, they enjoyed many of the blessings intended for the ultimate recipients of the promise*—possession of the land, God's special presence, national prestige, and prosperity. They could live off the interest.

165

If they disobeyed, they could expect disaster rather than blessing. The Law was God's way of guiding His people into a life-style He could bless. God gave them the Law because He loved them.

It worked . . . for a while. The generation that came out of Egypt promised to obey the Law. But they continued to resist God's will and finally pronounced sentence on themselves (Num. 14: 2). As a result, they wandered in the wilderness for thirty-eight years until that generation died. Their children, however, followed the Lord (Deut. 4: 4). After hearing a review of their history and a restatement of the Law of Moses (the Book of Deuteronomy), the purified people followed a new leader, Joshua, to conquer the promised land of Canaan.

The next books of the Old Testament (Joshua, Judges), and the 400 or so years of history they record, demonstrate the twin themes of obedience and victory, disobedience and defeat.

During the days of Joshua, the people followed God and won victory after victory (after an interlude in which one man's sin caused the defeat of the whole people; see Josh. 7—8).

Even though they, too, committed themselves to the Covenant of Law (see Josh. 24: 14-28), the Hebrew people in the next centuries fell into idolatry and disobedience, losing sight of God. The Book of Judges describes these times and shows how succeeding generations fell into sin, only to know God's judgment through conquering enemies.

When the people returned to God, He would raise up a judge (both a military and political leader) to

166

deliver them. But after a time of peace, the people would again turn away. Judges 17—21 shows the inevitable results of refusing to live by God's laws. Only the little Book of Ruth, relating events that happened during the times of the judges, gives a glimmer of light and reminds us that individuals can live for the Lord even when the society around them is corrupt.

For us. We may not be under Law as were the Israelites (Rom 6:14). But disobedience to God's revealed will can still bring us harm. God loves us, and in love He tells us how to live. He shows us what will help us and what will harm us. He cares enough to let us know what's best for us.

How good if we will learn from Israel's experience and choose to do God's will before we experience the sorrow and suffering that sin must ultimately bring.

And how good to know we have a God who cares, a God who is holy and just and good, a God who wants His children to be like Him. We choose to obey because we love God, and want His best.

KING AND KINGDOM
Date: 1050-722 B.C.
Text: 1, 2 Samuel; 1, 2 Kings; 1, 2 Chronicles; Psalms; Proverbs; Ecclesiastes
Events: a kingdom established . . . and divided
To sample, read: 2 Sam. 7 (God's plan involves a Jewish king?). 1 Kings 12:25—13:10 (Sometimes leaders are why people go bad). 2 Chron. 29—31 (Then again, leaders can be good!). Ps.

167

23 (All this time, people could have had a deep, personal relationship with God—just like now).

A fresh beginning. People had had enough of judges and personal responsibility. They wanted what other nations had: a strong leader to lead their battles and set the tone of the country. So, even though the people's motives were wrong, God gave Israel yet another fresh start. He established a monarchy.

Three kings. Under the first three kings of Israel, a strong, united nation was developed. Saul, the first king, proved to be a weak man. Instead of leading the people to obey God, he followed the people and disobeyed God (1 Sam. 13; 15).

David, the next king, was a truly godly man. He wasn't perfect, but he was quick to confess his sins and rely on God's forgiveness (Pss. 32; 51). He wanted to obey God, because he loved Him. David expressed his love and faith in many psalms, which were used for public worship in Israel. He increased the land holdings of Israel ten times over, set up a strong, centralized government, reestablished the worship of God according to the decrees in Exodus and Leviticus, and became the true father of his country.

Solomon, David's son, continued to build by diplomacy what David had won by military might. Under Solomon, Israel became fantastically wealthy—yet the people were heavily taxed. Solomon collected and wrote many of the proverbs in our Bible, and during his later days he wrote

Ecclesiastes. He began his reign well (see 2 Chron. 6—7), but later he drifted away from God (1 Kings 11).

A good start such as Solomon had is important, but it's keeping on the road all the way that counts. Solomon was in many ways a dismal failure.

Crack-up! After Solomon's death in 931 B.C., the kingdom built by David broke in two. A northern kingdom, called Israel, included ten of the twelve tribes that had made up the nation. A southern kingdom, called Judah, retained the two other tribes along with those individuals who crossed over the border so they could continue to worship in Jerusalem.

Israel (the Northern Kingdom) was ruled by a series of kings who rejected God and His ways. The first king, Jeroboam, wanted to keep his people from going to Jerusalem to worship. So he set up a system of false worship, with substitute sacrifices and an unauthorized priesthood. He and subsequent kings were marked by moral weaknesses and gross sins. Even though God sent prophets to warn the people of Israel (see the next section), they sinned more and more. Finally, in 722 B.C., God permitted the Assyrians under Sargon II to capture the kingdom and deport the people. The warnings given by Moses (Deut. 28) had come true.

Judah (the Southern Kingdom) had mixed leadership. There were several godly kings and times of revival. But the same sins that scarred Israel existed in Judah. There was immorality and injustice. There was idolatry and pagan worship. There was

169

open breaking of God's laws, perjury, and fraud. The fall of Israel should have been an object lesson to Judah. But the people disregarded this warning just as they disregarded the prophets God sent. Finally, Judah too was overwhelmed by the Babylonians and, in a series of deportations, the people were removed from their land. Jerusalem, including Solomon's magnificent Temple, was burned. Refusal to obey God's Law had led inevitably to disaster.

The King ahead. Strong leadership had not been the answer. The leaders had been too much like the people: flawed, human, sinful. Even the best were unable to bring in the kind of righteousness that God's Law shows He requires.

But the days of the kings reveal another facet of God's plan. In God's promise to David (2 Sam. 7), often called the Davidic Covenant, God promised that a descendant of David would rule the world forever! God promised Abraham to bless the world through him. Now we see that to fulfill that promise, God will anoint a King.

The rest of the Bible speaks much about the coming King. This King will "judge the poor with justice and defend the humble in the land with equity; his mouth shall be a rod to strike down the ruthless, and with a word He shall slay the wicked" (Isa. 11:4, New English Bible). The coming King will bring in the righteousness and justice that the Law reveals are a part of God's own character, and thus a part of His plan for man. None of the kings of the Old Testament days could do this. But *the* coming King will.

And who is this King? To make it perfectly clear, both Matthew (chapter 1) and Luke (chapter 3) trace the genealogy of one man, Jesus Christ. They show that He is David's descendant. He is the rightful King of Israel, and of the world.

Someday Jesus is coming back to our earth. When He does, it won't be as a helpless baby. It will be as a mighty, ruling King. In that day all the promises made to Abraham and David will be kept. And in that day, our earth will know what righteousness is.

❧

PROPHETS SPEAK
Date: 931-586 B.C.
Text: Major and Minor Prophets
Events: Division . . . and drift
To sample, read: Amos 6; Isa. 1 (What did God get so angry about? Amos 9: 9-15 (How about that Covenant?). Isa. 11: 6-10 (What else did the prophets say about the future?). Hab. (Here's a three-chapter prophecy you'll enjoy).

Warning! Warning! Seeing how life deteriorated into sin and idolatry under the kings of Israel and Judah, one wonders why God didn't do something.

He did! What He did was to speak to His people through the written Scriptures and through men whom He commissioned, the prophets.

These men communicated God's special messages to His people at critical points in history. Some, like Elijah (see 1 Kings 17—21) and Elisha (2 Kings 2—9), spoke but did not write their messages.

171

Others, such as Isaiah, Amos, and Jeremiah, not only ministered to their own generation but were used by God to add books to our Bible.

In order to authenticate a man as His messenger, God would foretell future events through him. A prophet would indicate what was going to happen in a short time (see 2 Kings 7), so people of his day would know he spoke God's words. He would also tell of things to happen decades or even thousands of years in the future—so that *we* can know he spoke God's words.

When a prophet unerringly told what the future would hold, the people of his day knew his message came from God. God did do something when His people slipped off into sin. He warned them, gave them fresh promises, explained His ways over and over. When kings and people would not listen, the tragic results of their sinful course were clearly their own fault.

It's like this with us. We can't blame God when we choose our own way, and then things don't work out as we wanted. The Bible makes God's way clear, and all of the Old Testament stands as a warning that turning away from God brings us harm and hurt. God loves us. He knows the best way—and tells us.

Color it in. The prophets spoke to their own people with promises and warnings. They also revealed more and more of God's plan, how He would some-day keep the promise made to Abraham. The early books of the Bible may be compared with drawings such as one finds in coloring books; the prophecies are as if one used crayons and colored the pictures.

As we read the books of the prophets and distinguish which prophecies were "near" (fulfilled soon after they were given) and which were "far" (fulfilled much later), we are fascinated by the wealth of detail added to the original promise God gave to Abraham. But who were the prophets, and why did they speak out?

Some prophets spoke primarily to the evil Northern Kingdom, Israel. *Jonah's* ministry to Nineveh shows that God will remit the punishment of a people who repent. *Obadiah* declares that God will judge those who hurt His people. *Amos* portrays the wealth and wickedness of Israel under Omri and promises judgment. *Hosea* pictures God as a betrayed husband who will rescue Israel from her adulterous involvement in idolatry, though he warns that the rescue will involve suffering.

God sent other prophets primarily to Judah, warning against the same sins that destroyed Israel. The good kings had been unable to effect real revival. *Micah* announces individual pardon, even though the nation will be judged. *Joel* gives a graphic picture of the judgment and destruction God will bring on His people if they will not repent. *Isaiah* is full of new revelations, including the coming King (Messiah) and His death for sinners. Isaiah also pictures the Kingdom of peace the Messiah will establish.

After Israel was carried into captivity in 722 B.C., Judah remained in Palestine. But she drifted deeper into sin. More prophets were sent: *Nahum* comforts those who fear Assyria (the conqueror of Israel) by promising its destruction. *Zephaniah* pictures God's judgment approaching. *Habakkuk* explores the nature of sin and God's use of a sinful people to chastise Judah. He warns that the great judgment of Judah is near. *Jeremiah* details the sinfulness of Judah's leaders and people before she, like Israel, was removed from the Promised Land. Yet even amid the gloom of judgment, God's promises are repeated and fresh promises given.

Look up! Looking around, a godly Jew could only have seen gloom. Looking up to God, he could find hope. For example, in Jeremiah 31—33 God restates the old promises and adds a new one. "I will put my law within them, and I will write it upon their hearts" (Jer. 31:33). God would enable His people to respond to Him by offering them a new heart, conversion.

It's the same with us. Maybe you've struggled to do what's right, and failed. Or maybe you've gladly chosen what you know is wrong. If so, there's still hope. God tells of a New Covenant, a promise He made when Jesus died (another "covenant of blood"). If you trust Jesus, Israel's Savior and King, God will change your heart. He'll make you a new person (2 Cor. 5:17) and free you to love and obey Him.

YEARS IN CHAINS
Date: 586-538 B.C.
Text: Jeremiah, Ezekiel, Daniel, Lamentations
Events: deportation; destruction of Jerusalem

To sample, read· Ezek. 8—11 (Was God's presence in the Temple when it burned? Why?). Jer. 42—43 (Had the people who were left in Judah learned their lesson?). Dan. 1—4 (God can use us in the most difficult situation). Dan. 7 (a fantastic view of what's ahead).

Captivity. I found a dish of peas in the refrigerator the other day, hidden behind some other containers. Looking in, I could see it was too late. Mold. And corruption. There was just one thing to do. I threw them out, fast!

When I look at the attitudes and actions of God's people just before Judah's captivity, I'm reminded of that dish of peas. Corrupt. Spoiled. We realize how spoiled they were when we look into some key passages.

Ezekiel was a young man of the priestly line who was carried away in the first of three deportations (606 B.C.). From Babylon, Ezekiel warned the other captives to settle down for a long stay, for God would destroy Judah and the Jerusalem Temple as well. The people wouldn't believe him. God couldn't destroy that Temple; it meant too much to Him! In a vision, Ezekiel is taken by God to Jerusalem, where he sees the sins that force God to remove His presence from His people and the Temple.

As Ezekiel foretells, Nebuchadnezzar's armies return and destroy city and Temple. Sin has devastated God's people.

Worth it all. Punishment always seems painful and hard. No child likes to be spanked. No adult likes

175

discipline. But punishment should have a purpose—and it always does when God administers it.

The Jews learned several important lessons during the Babylonian Captivity. First, they were purged from the sin of idolatry. Before this time, generation after generation had fallen into idol worship and the gross immoralities that normally accompany it. No more.

The people also turned back to the Word of God. They set up synagogues and assembled to read and talk about the Bible. Men began to devote their lives to reading and studying the Bible and became rabbis (teachers). Throughout the rest of Jewish history, the study of God's Law and the teaching of it has had a central place.

After some seventy years of captivity in Babylon, the Jews returned to their land. They were equipped to make another fresh start. God was giving them another chance to be true to Him so they could enjoy the blessings He promised through the Law to His Covenant people.

Meanwhile. Even in Babylon, God used men who remained faithful to Him. Daniel was one of these men, and his book is one that can help anyone in a tough situation.

God spoke through the prophet Daniel to tell His people more about their future. The Jews would not have another king of their own until Messiah came, but would be under a succession of Gentile world powers. By means of the information given in Daniel and in the New Testament Book of Revelation, believers have developed a striking picture of Christ's return as King of Kings and Lord of Lords.

The Captivity was not the end; it was a part of God's care for His own. When its purposes were achieved, God brought His people home.

THE BOOK CLOSED

Date: 538-400 B.C.
Text: Ezra, Nehemiah, Esther, Haggai, Zechariah, Malachi
Events: return, rebuilding
To sample, read: Neh. 8; 13 (It was a great day when the city was rebuilt. But how long did revival last?). Zech. 12—14 (Have God's plans been sidetracked? Here it is: the big picture loud and clear). Mal. (Look through this last book of the Old Testament. Things always get better, don't they?).

The end? The Captivity in Babylon served its purpose. Then God brought His people back to the Promised Land, at least those who wanted to come (Ezra 1: 5). It was a fresh start for people who really wanted to follow the Lord.

The Old Testament seems full of fresh starts. This time, too, there were strong leaders to help God's people. Ezra and Nehemiah were the counterparts of Moses and David. The first group of Jews returned in 538 B.C. (Ezra 1—6). Another group returned fifty-eight years later under Ezra's leadership (7: 27—10: 44). The final return occurred still later under Nehemiah. The Temple was rebuilt, and finally the city walls were rebuilt as well.

These were years of struggle for the Jewish people. They were colonists now in their own land, and they faced opposition from surrounding peoples as well as the barrenness of a countryside razed by wars. But again God sent encouragement. *Haggai*, a prophet, urged the people to complete the rebuilding of God's house. Unlike the people before the Exile, this generation listened! They did as the prophet urged, and the Temple was finished with great rejoicing.

Meanwhile, back in the capital of the Persian Empire, which had overthrown the Babylonian Empire during the days of Daniel, a plot to destroy the whole Jewish people developed. Haman, a court official in the Persian capital, obtained a decree for the Jews' destruction, only to be thwarted by a woman. The Book of *Esther* helps us see that God was still caring for His people (and that women have an important place in His plans).

Zechariah told the Jews that they must live under Gentile rule for a time. Then, after further purging, the promised King would come.

Same new story. Probably the most striking thing about these post exilic books is that we find in them the same themes we saw in earlier prophecies. The people still sinned. And still were warned. The King was still to come. After war, holocaust, and judgment, the King, present at last, would begin His rule. The days of peace would be at hand.

In the meantime? *Malachi* tells us what happened.

Once again the new start failed. Within a generation or two, the people of God were bickering, selfish, and hardhearted toward God and one another. The Old Testament ends on this note of defeat and the warning of judgment. If this were truly the end, humanity would have no hope.

CROSS . . . AND CROWN
Text: the whole Old Testament
Events: prophecies concerning Jesus
To sample, read: Isa. 9: 6-7 (Who is the coming King?). Mic. 5: 2; Isa. 7: 14; Zech. 9: 9 (Do we have details?). Psa. 22; Isa. 53 (Was He really to suffer? Take a look at the last book of the New Testament—Rev. 19, for instance. He *is* coming as King!).

King Jesus. The Old Testament ends on a note of despair. Each time God's people have started on the path of obedience, they have failed.

It's not that God hasn't helped. He gave them a number of fresh starts. He gave them strong, godly men to lead them. He gave them His Word to guide them. He gave them prophets to warn and encourage them. He fought for them and gave them victory over enemies much more powerful than they. Why then did the grand experiment seem to fail?

A grim lesson. The early chapters of Genesis explain the course of subsequent Bible history. When God warned Adam and Eve that spiritual and physical death must inevitably follow sin, the couple did not realize what the lasting impact of that death would be. We find it hard to realize even today. Yet the complete inability of Israel to follow God and live His way helps us see what sin is and does.

Sin isn't just that little white lie or even that act of viciousness. Sin is a twisting of the human personality, a twisting that results in people and nations inevitably resisting God and His ways. They choose evil even when they know it will destroy them! Sin is the destroyer of hope, polluter of love, dasher of dreams. Sin is something that has to be faced, because if not dealt with it will destroy you.

A promise unfolds. As it became clear that nothing God or man could do about circumstances could bring peace and justice, God also made it clear that He intended to do something about man's character. Sin, the cause of suffering, would be dealt with.

From the very first, God taught that sin could only be dealt with by death. When Adam and Eve sinned, God killed an animal to provide a skin covering for their nakedness and shame (Gen. 3:21). Cain was angry because God insisted on a blood sacrifice (Gen. 4:3), and, in his anger, he lashed out to kill his brother. The blood on the doorposts in Egypt at the time of the first Passover and the whole system of sacrifices instituted at Sinai taught and retaught the single lesson: sin deserves death. Remission of your sin requires that another must die in your place.

As the centuries passed, God began to reveal who it was that would ultimately die for sin. Through Isaiah, God made it very clear. The coming King would be "wounded for our transgressions." He would "make many righteous" by bearing their iniquities (chap. 53).

As Old and New Testaments agree, the death of Jesus marked the making of a New Covenant. That promise focused on renewing the human heart (Jer. 31:31-34; Heb. 8:6-12). Through His death, the King changes people from *within* and frees us from the warping power of sin that otherwise dominates us.

Savior-King. So two lines of prophecy blend. God would provide a King. God would provide a Savior.

And who would this Savior-King be? Isaiah says it again: "You shall call His name Immanuel" (Isa. 7:14). Many prophets speak of His resurrection. Many tell of His everlasting reign (and thus His endless life). Many state that His rule will be the rule of God Himself. Yes, the son of David will also be Son of God.

This must have been hard for the Old Testament saints to understand, if indeed they did. But from the perspective of history, we can understand. In Palestine some two thousand years ago, a baby was born. As He grew into manhood, He began to teach and do miracles. His message about Himself was clear. He was the promised King, the promised Savior. God appeared in human flesh to deal once and for all with sin. On His cross He *did* deal with sin. And soon, when He comes again, He will take up His crown.

He will keep the promises God made to Abraham so long ago. For God always keeps His promises. That's the kind of person He is.

GOING DEEPER

to personalize

Select one period of Old Testament history reviewed in this chapter and read the recommended sample passages. Be ready to share in class truths which seem especially meaningful to you.

to probe

As a framework for understanding Old Testament history, memorize the data given in each section heading in the chapter.

13

KEY CHAPTERS

THE OLD TESTAMENT, together with the New, provides the foundation of our faith. The Old Testament has a number of keystone chapters that contain pivotal truths. We can turn to them to review the central teachings of this part of the Bible. Other chapters have great personal impact. In these lifestyle chapters we find a special word of comfort or guidance concerning our personal lives and needs. The following lists of both kinds of chapters will be a handy reference for future reading in the Old Testament.

KEYSTONE CHAPTERS

Chapter	Theme	Study Questions
Exod. 3	Moses' call	Who does God reveal Himself to be? What gives Moses confidence in his mission?
Exod. 6—11	Mighty acts	What actions does God take on behalf of His people? What are His motives?
Exod. 12	Passover	What is the significance of this feast? Why is it important for God's people to remember?
Exod. 14	Red Sea	This event is referred to many times in the Old Testament. In what ways does it symbolize deliverance?
Exod. 20	Ten Commandments	What do they reveal about God? How can they help us?
Lev. 10	Aaron's priesthood	What was the mission of the priests? How do we know their ministry was important and holy?

Lev. 16	Blood sacrifice	How was sin to be atoned for (covered)?
Lev. 19	Holiness	What is God's goal for His people? How does He want us to live?
Num. 14	Wilderness wanderings	Why didn't God's people immediately enter the Promised Land?
Deut. 6	God's Word	How can we communicate God's Word so He is real to others?
Deut. 18	Prophets	What will be the role of prophets in Israel? How can a prophet be recognized?
Deut. 28	Warnings	In what ways did these warnings and promises come to pass in Israel's later history?
Josh. 1	Conquest	What promise does God give Joshua? What must he do?
Judg. 1	Decline	Why did Israel weaken after settling in the Promised Land? What were God's motives in judging her?

1 Sam. 8	Monarchy	Why did God's people want a king? Was this a good choice for them?
2 Sam. 7	Davidic Covenant	What does God promise David?
1 Kings 8	Temple	What were Solomon's motives in building the Jerusalem Temple? What does his prayer tell us of its function in Old Testament worship?
1 Kings 12	Kingdom divided	What were the spiritual principles on which the Northern Kingdom, Israel, was based? How might this explain that through its history (931-722) Israel had no godly rulers?
2 Kings 17	Israel destroyed	What were the causes of Israel's defeat?
2 Chron. 36	Judah's Captivity	Why was Judah defeated and carried into captivity?
Isa. 1	Indictment	What sins caused God to act in judgment against His people?

Isa. 53	Messiah	How will Messiah deliver us from sin?
Jer. 31	New Covenant	What Covenant (agreement) will be replaced? What will the New Covenant include?
Ezek. 18	Individual judgment	Does God deal only with nations, or does He distinguish between individuals as He judges?
Ezek. 37	Restoration	What will the time of restoration be like? What is involved for Israel?
Dan. 7	Gentile times	What will happen between the Babylonian Captivity and the restoration?
Amos 5	Justice	What is the nature of justice? How is justice expressed in society?
Ezra 3	Return	What did the Jews do when they returned from captivity in Babylon? What were their motives?
Neh. 8	The Word	While they were in captivity, the Jews returned to Scripture. What place does the Bible have in their lives now?

LIFE-STYLE CHAPTERS

Chapters	Theme	Application
Gen. 3	Temptation	Examine how Satan approaches temptation.
Gen. 17	Faith	What is impossible for us is possible for God. Faith is trusting and acting on God's Word.
Gen. 27	Anxiety	Jacob had been promised the Covenant birthright. But he and his mother were anxious and plotted to get what God would have freely given. The results are a lesson for us!
Gen. 45	Injustice	Joseph suffered an injustice from his brothers. But he kept on doing right in his difficult situation. His insight is important when we're treated unfairly.
Exod. 20	Morality	Morality is rooted in the character of God. Here's how we car become more like Him.

Lev. 26	Obedience	God's laws guide us into the path of blessing.
Num. 11	Discontent	Israel had the very presence of God but was not content with Him or His blessings. Discontent can lead us into difficulties!
Deut. 7	Sense of identity	We are God's people too, called to live with and for Him.
Deut. 11	Love	The Bible always links love and obedience (or responsiveness). Here's how.
Deut 30	Commitment	The choices we make are significant. Our decisions determine the course of our lives.
1 Sam. 17	Courage	David's willingness to face Goliath is an example for us. If God is with us, no enemy is too powerful.
1 Sam. 24	Restraint	David was unwilling to kill Saul when the opportunity came. He determined to do only what was right.

2 Sam. 22	Praise	When God helps us, it is appropriate to rejoice and to praise Him. Here's a fine example of praise.
Ps. 23	Peace	Because God is our shepherd, we can have rest.
Ps. 31	Fear	Here is David's own deep sense of God as his refuge.
Ps. 51	Failure	David's psalm of confession gives us a model when we sin and fail God.
Ps. 69	Desperation	No extremity is too great. We can call on God with confidence.
Ps. 73	Envy	What happens when you see the wicked doing well, and you're troubled on every side?
Ps. 104	Praise	How do we thank and praise God?
Ps. 119	Motivation	What is our greatest desire? How does Scripture aid us?
Prov. 3	Uncertainty	God's wisdom provides the guidance we need.

Isa. 44	Assurance	It helps to remember just who God is, and to rest our confidence in Him.
Jer. 34	Faithfulness	God expects His people to be obedient.
Dan. 1	Pressured	Daniel was. And he found the only way out.
Hos. 11	Shame	God never gives up on us.
Hab. 3	Danger	Habakkuk was afraid. But he found faith.

Many other passages and chapters in the writings of the Old Testament will come to have meaning for you. It's a great privilege to read, to be strengthened and comforted, and to make even greater discoveries as God speaks to us.

GOING DEEPER

to personalize

1. There's great value in reading through the Old Testament and making a record of chapters or passages that speak especially to us. Make your own record of short passages from Isaiah that have taken on special meaning to you during these studies.

2. Or choose three passages from the lists in this chapter. Read them carefully, and write briefly on their value to you personally.

to probe

Begin a "discovery diary." Start now to read through the Old Testament, a few chapters a day. Record in your diary special chapters or passages that take on meaning for you.